From Religion to Christianity

THE PROCESS OF TRANSFORMATION INTO THE NATURE OF CHRIST

CST CHIGWADA

From Religion to Christianity

Copyright © 2016 by CST Chigwada

Published by **Christ In Me Publishing**

First Edition
ISBN-13 978-0-9955474-0-7 (Paperback)
ISBN-13 978-0-9955474-1-4 (ebook-Mobi)
ISBN-13 978-0-9955474-2-1 (ebook-epub)

Printed in the United Kingdom
and the United States of America

Cover and interior design by Vanessa Mendozzi

To request CST Chigwada for teaching, training, speaking engagements, or interviews, please send an email to:
cleopas.chigwada@yahoo.co.uk

CST Chigwada's books are available at special discounts when purchased in bulk as a Spiritual Growth tool for Churches or as donations for educational and Ministry training purposes.

Limit of Liability/Disclaimer of Warranty

Dedication

I would like to dedicate this book to my three lovely daughters — Nyaradzo, Nyasha, and Rufaro, and my late father, Evangelist Aaron Tirivanhu Chigwada.

Acknowledgments

I would like to thank the team that worked very hard behind the scenes typing, editing, and designing to produce this book: Kevin Robinson, Zandi Dube, Davison Sedze and the publishing consultant - Victor Kwegyir a very professional hard working man. But above everyone else, I would like to thank God, who makes me have the will and ability to do His Will.

Contents

Preface

From Religion to Christianity is a book deliberately written in very simple language for all to understand. This is because of the great importance of the message in it, which all must understand. To further show the importance of this message, some aspects of the book are repeated a few times.

What is this important message that all must hear? Together, let us look at the introduction of this book, where this very important message appears for the first time.

C.S.T. CHIGWADA

London, 2015

Introduction

Welcome to *From Religion to Christianity*.

This is a book for all people. This book is based on the true living God. God does not change, but His ways of dealing with people changes with time. Reading through the Bible will show you the change in God's dealings with people at various times in biblical history.

The picture we see as we read through the Bible is that some things that were the truth at one time are no longer the truth today. From this, we can talk about 'Old Truth' and 'New Truth'. 'Old Truth' had an important role to play in its own time; does this mean that 'Old Truth' has no role to play today?

No. 'Old Truth' has a role to play today, as is clearly shown in this book. The Bible also clearly shows us what was never meant to be the role of the 'Old Truth'. Are there Christians today who are still holding onto the 'Old Truth' and holding it — or some aspects of it — up as the pillar of their faith?

This, I am sure, does help us to explain why some Christians' lifestyle is spiritually stunted, while others are giants spiritually.

From this we can classify Christians into three groups:

- Those with a Christian lifestyle based on the old Biblical truth.
- Those with a Christian lifestyle based on a mixture of the old truth and new truth.
- Those with a Christian lifestyle based on new truth.

NOTE: In which group do you think you are operating as a Christian? Join me as we explore the Bible to find out what the old Biblical truth is and what the new Biblical truth is. And more importantly, what is walking in step with God? Or as Galatians 2:14 puts it, what is walking in the truth of the gospel?

CHAPTER 1

The Dispensations of God

"Through him all things were made; without him, nothing was made that has been made." — John 1:3

The Bible tells us that it was God who created all things and that He created them for Himself. In Genesis, the very first book of the Bible, we see God in the process of creation. The story of creation is found in Chapters One and Two of the book of Genesis. Man was created at the very end of the process and placed in the Garden of Eden. A closer look at the life of man on earth from the Bible's point of view shows that, from creation up to the present time, God has been dealing with people in different ways from one era to another.

God Himself does not change, but the way He deals with people varies from time to time.

NOTE: A political, religious or social system prevailing at a particular time is called a 'dispensation'.

So the way God administers His affairs or deals with people at a particular time is called a dispensation. A close look at the history of God's earthly chosen people, the Jews, clearly shows the idea of a dispensation. The diagram below illustrates God's dispensation.

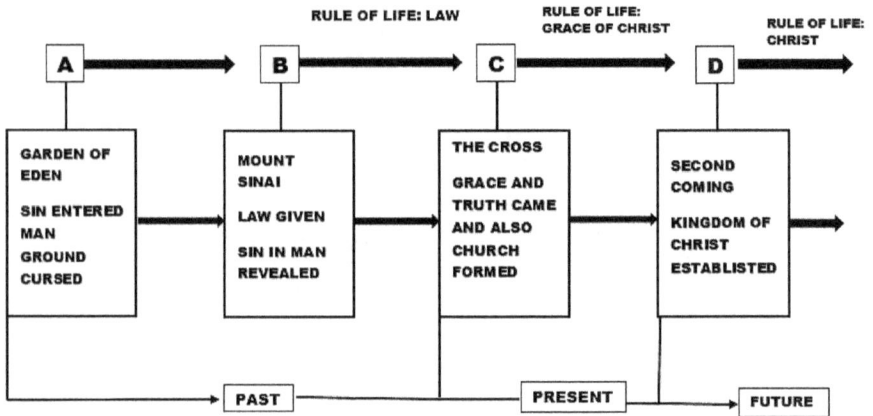

Key features of the above diagram:

A) **Garden of Eden**
Man created and depended on God for everything.
Sin entered man, and the ground was cursed.

B) **Mount Sinai**
Law given by God through Moses to the Jews: the Law (moral and ceremonial law) is the same thing as the 'Old Covenant', or what is generally referred to as the Ten Commandments.

Purpose of the Law: To show that people are sinners and the need for the Saviour. The Law became the rule of life for that era.

C) **The Cross**
Jesus Christ came, died, and rose again. He brought grace and truth.

The church was formed by the work of the Holy Spirit. The church was to exist from Pentecost to Rapture. Grace/Christ became the rule of life. The solution to our sinful nature was made known to the people. This is the present.

D) The Second Coming

This is the future. Christ is coming to establish His kingdom and reign together with the saints. The Second Coming is divided into two parts. The first part is the Rapture, when Christ comes to take believers — dead and alive — to heaven; during that time, awards are made to saints, in what is referred to as the Judgment Seat of Christ/Bema Seat of Christ (1 Thessalonians 4:16-18).

The second part is when Christ comes to earth with the believers (saints) to establish His kingdom and reign for a thousand years. This period is referred to as the Millennium/The day of The Lord/The Revelation.

2 Thessalonians 1:7-9
2 Thessalonians 2:1-12

Revelations Chapters 4-22

This is the time for tribulation and judgment for those who refuse to believe in Jesus Christ. This is also the time when the new covenant will be completely fulfilled and the nation of Israel will be restored and blessed. A comparison of two different periods of the above diagram will also bring out some interesting things about how God deals with his people from one era to another.

Period B-C: Mt. Sinai to the Cross	Period C-D: The Cross to the Second Coming
A) Law rule of life	A) Christ (Grace) rule of life
B) Certain foods looked at as unclean. (Leviticus 11)	B) All foods clean (1 Timothy 4:3-4; Colossians 2:16-17)
C) Circumcision a must for all Jewish males	C) Circumcision is not significant (Galatians 6:15)
D) Keeping the Sabbath a must for the Jews (Exodus 31:12-13)	D) Keeping the Sabbath not a must for Christians (Colossians 2:16-17)
E) Emphasis in this era is what men must do. It is about *you* and what *you* should be doing. Emphasis is on man and religion	E) Emphasis is on *God*. All has been done, the finished work. The *you* has been replaced by *I*, referring to God's actions. (Hebrews 8:10-12)

The table above shows that what God wanted people to do in one era does not apply and has no significance in the next era. Does this mean that we should not preach about that which does not apply to the present-day dispensation of God? Does this not show inconsistency in the Bible? The answer to both questions is 'No — not at all'. We must preach, teach, and study every part of the Bible; there is consistency in the whole Bible.

We should preach from the Old Testament as well as the New Testament, but the emphasis in all preaching is to help people see Christ in all the scriptures. See Luke 24:25-27 and Hebrews 10:7. These two readings show that we are justified in looking for Jesus in all the scriptures and that seeing Jesus in all the scriptures pleases God.

Pictures/Shadows of Christ	Bible Readings
Melchizedek: King/priest	Genesis 14:18-20
Joseph: Forgiving his brothers	Genesis 50:15-26
Moses: Deliverer of the Jews	Exodus Chapter 3
Manna: Bread of life	Exodus 16:25
Esther: Submission and dependence	Esther 2:20 and 54
Boaz: Kinsman redeemer	Ruth 4:13-14
Mercy seat: Atonement cover	Exodus 37:6-7

Do we see pictures of Christ as we read through the Old Testament? For example, when we read about offerings in the book of Leviticus or keeping the Sabbath, or about the tabernacle and all that was in it, like the Ark of The Covenant as we read the book of Exodus? These are what the Bible calls pictures or shadows (typology) of Christ — things that represented Christ and things that acted as pointers to Christ (Colossians 2:16-17).

So, why do we see people who belong to the Dispensation of Grace still clinging to the things that belong to the Dispensation of Law? Some people would rather keep the Sabbath (Law) than enter the Sabbath rest, which is just trusting and relying on Christ (Grace). Keeping the Sabbath is human effort. Entering the Sabbath rest involves you trusting and relying on God for things to be done (Hebrews 4: 9-10).

I believe the major reason that people still cling to shadows is that people seem to get more satisfaction and confidence in perfor-mance-based lifestyles — in doing things themselves rather than in believing in God. The question is: Is it not a sin to cling to shadows, when you know Christ has come? This is a sin because, in a way, this person is saying the finished work of Christ is not sufficient in making the person a true Christian. The other reason is wrong teaching/preaching, which results in mixing of Grace (New Truth) and the Law (Old Truth).

Unfortunately, when we depend on ourselves, we will have no power to resist the devil, and, as a result, the devil ends up reigning in peoples' lives. This is not God's plan for mankind. God wants us to trust and rely on Him in all things. This is the best for us — not a human-performance-based lifestyle. The sad thing today is that some people have moved on to engage in performance-based type of christianity, for example, intellectualising and rationalising the Gospel, giving money to the poor, attending church or wearing a church uniform as a way of getting a right standing before God. This makes Christ of no value. If Christ is of no value, then there is no Christianity — because Christianity is all about *Christ*.

The Lord, as the Saviour of mankind, is the constant feature in the whole Bible and through all the Dispensations. From Genesis to Revelation, we see that people are saved only when they believe in God and not by works (human effort). "Abraham believed God, and it was accounted to him for righteousness" (Romans 4:3). The same is true today: We are saved by grace through faith in Jesus Christ only (Ephesians 2:8).

We have seen that the only constant feature in the all the dispensa-tions from Genesis to Revelation is Christ. Today people ask, 'What is the significance of Jesus Christ appearing throughout the Bible, and is there any difference in people's lives today between knowing Him and not knowing Him? Let us answer this question: Why Jesus Christ?

CHAPTER 2

Why Believe in Jesus Christ?

"This is my son whom I love; listen to him." — Luke 9:35.

These are the words of God referring to Jesus Christ. In John 3:16-17, the Bible says, *"For God so loved the world that he gave his only son, that whoever believes in him should not perish but have everlasting life. For God did not send his son into the world to condemn the world but that the world through him might be saved."* These Biblical quotations show that Jesus Christ was sent by God into the world to carry out very important tasks for the benefit of mankind and that, without Jesus Christ, mankind will never overcome that problem; without Christ, mankind will never become what God created them to be.

Who is Jesus? Why did he come? What did he do for mankind? What is He going to do for us today?

Before we go much further, we also need to find out what the Apostle Paul said about Jesus in the thirteen books of the New Testament that he wrote.

Paul shows that, in the person of Christ, God — who is invisible but made Himself visible to mankind and to the believers in particular, also through Christ — revealed His love of mankind. This is the true nature of our God.

In all his thirteen books in the Bible, Paul is constantly referring his readers to the *person of Christ*. See the following Bible passages: 1 Corinthians 1:23-24; Colossians 1:27; Colossians 2:9; 1 Timothy 2:3-7; and Titus 2:13-14. Just from these few passages, we see that Paul, in all his writings, is trying to show his readers about the supremacy and the all-sufficiency of our Lord Jesus Christ to give believers all that is needed for life and Godliness. In what way does Christ show His all-sufficiency in the life of a believer?

God created man in His own image (just like a glove made in the image of the human hand), so that God could come into man, live in man, and express himself through man. But this did not happen at that time, because sin entered man, making it impossible for the righteous God to come into the unrighteous man. But this did not stop God's plan to enter and live in man. God became a man (the process of incarnation) — and came to live in this world as a person who was 100% man and 100% God — called Jesus Christ.

In the Bible, Jesus Christ is referred to by many different names and titles. Some of these names are: The Lamb of God; Son of God; Son of Man; The Redeemer; Emmanuel; The Bread of Life; The Way, The Truth and the Life; The Prince of Peace; The Light of the World; The King of Kings; The Mighty God, Everlasting.

The name 'Jesus Christ' does not appear as such in the Old Testament. We come across it only in the New Testament. In the Old Testament, Jesus appears under other names, such as Wonderful

Counsellor, Servant of God, Man of Sorrow, etc. or He appears in the Old Testament concealed as a picture or shadow (see Colossians 2:16-17 and Hebrews 10:1). So, we see Jesus Christ in the whole Bible. In the Old Testament, we see Him in a concealed form, and in the New Testament, we see Him in real form, as the fullness of the Godhead (Colossians 2:9).

The Bible describes Jesus as having unsearchable riches (Ephesians 3: 8). In what ways do we see the riches of Christ? The many names and titles given to Jesus show the many roles and functions Jesus came to perform for mankind. For example, as the Lamb of God, he died on our behalf as sinners fit for death. His death satisfied God's requirements for our justification and for us to receive his gift of righteousness and all other blessings, like the gift of no condemnation, the spirit of God, the life of God — making believers children of God. *His Grace = salvation.*

The work of Christ on the cross is described as the finished work (see John 19:30). It is the finished work because it qualifies believers to just believe and receive from god. For example, blessings for believers are by believing and receiving and not by human effort. Because of the finished work, man's greatest problem, his sinful nature, is dealt with differently today — by believing in Jesus Christ. In Old Testament times, it was dealt with by having a sinner bring a lamb with no defects to the priest, who would inspect the lamb to make sure it was perfect. Once the priest was satisfied, the sinner would touch the head of the lamb, and, by touching the head of the lamb, divine exchange was believed to take place. The sinner's sins would go into the lamb and the righteousness of the lamb would cover the sinner for a given time. See Hebrews 10:1-4 and Leviticus 1:1-4.

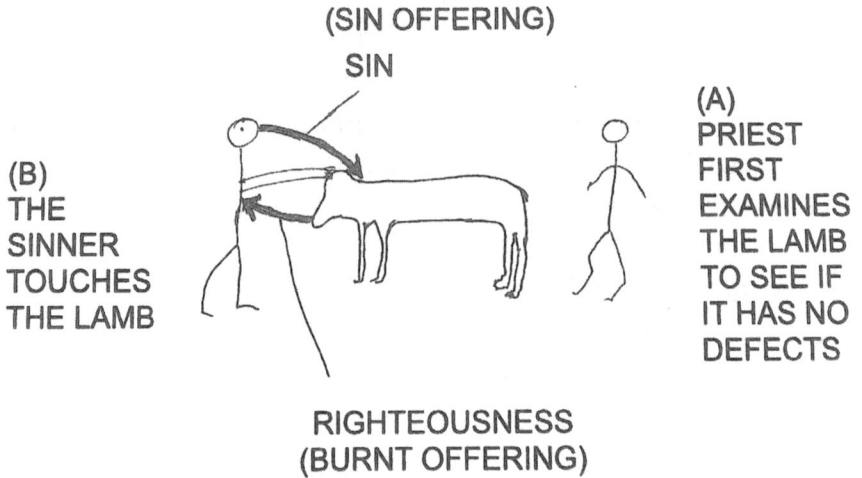

(SIN OFFERING)
SIN

(A)
PRIEST
FIRST
EXAMINES
THE LAMB
TO SEE IF
IT HAS NO
DEFECTS

(B)
THE
SINNER
TOUCHES
THE LAMB

RIGHTEOUSNESS
(BURNT OFFERING)

NOTE:

(1) The diagram adapted from: *Destined to Reign* by Joseph Prince.

(2) Christ came to take the place of all the offerings which were being done under the law.

This process was repeated several times in the life of a person. This was because the blood of animals could not take away the sins of a person. The blood only covered the sin for a limited period.

Today, Jesus is the perfect Lamb of God. When we believe in Him, what He accomplished for us through His finished work 2000 years ago becomes real in the life of the believer. His/her sins are taken away, and the believer is covered by the righteousness of God. This is divine exchange. Righteousness is again from God, and the only way to get it is by believing in Jesus Christ and not by works. There is no other way to remove sin from a person except through Jesus. There is no other way a person can have a right standing before God except through Jesus. It is only through Jesus we are reconciled to God. It is only through Jesus that we are reconciled to each other. It is only through Jesus that we were made into the new creation, the church (Ephesians 2:13-19).

In the book of Leviticus, we read about several types of offerings. Each one had its own specific requirements and was to be repeated several times in a year. They were not one-off things; this shows that these offerings were only God's temporary solution to man's sinful nature. They were a shadow of the good things that were coming. Jesus Christ is the reality (the perfect offering); the animal and the grain offering were only a shadow (Hebrews 10:1-4). Jesus Christ, the Lamb of God, came and took over the place of all the different types of offerings and feasts that we read about in the Bible, and His sacrifice on the cross was simply the final sacrifice, once and for all, taking away all our sins forever (Hebrews 7:26-27; Hebrews 10:1-12).

Our part today is to believe in Jesus Christ and to receive all that His finished work has accomplished for us. Today, Jesus is not only the Lamb of God to take away our sins — He is our Great High Priest, forever. He represents us before God and God to us; he is perfect and blameless, able to save us in the true and real sense — not like the blood of animals we read about in Leviticus.

"The priesthood of Jesus is not based on the law, but on the power of an indestructible life" (Hebrews 7:16 and Hebrews 9). Jesus is described as the source of external salvation for all who obey him. Salvation means saved from going to hell; salvation means healing, joy, peace, deliverance, protection, success and prosperity, power over sin, guidance and many more blessings.

The finished work of Jesus on the cross is really good news to us. Jesus Christ is the only solution to the world's deepest problem. What is this problem? It is the sinful nature of mankind. If you look very closely at the problems we read about in our newspapers or what we see on the television — things like terrorism, war, murder, economic problems, divorce, rape, human slavery, global warming — you will find that the sinful nature of mankind has something to do with each of the problems we are facing today. It all starts in the human heart of someone as greed, hatred, bitterness, jealousy, lust, envy, or selfishness, and, if nothing is done, in time, this internal evil, which is in the form of thoughts, ideas, and plans will be transformed into action.

Today we thank God for Jesus Christ: *"The grace of God that brings salvation has appeared to all man; it teaches us to say no to ungodliness and worldly passions, and today live self-controlled, upright, and godly lives in this present age."* (Titus 2:11-12)

The Gospel of Jesus Christ does not only make us know what sin is, but it also breaks the power of sin in us and over us, and we also are redeemed, pardoned, and forgiven for our sins. Jesus Christ *"... is the atoning sacrifice for our sins, and not only for ours but also for the sins of the world"* (1 John 2:2). It empowers believers to resist sin and to live Christ-like lives. Amen — this is what the Law could not do.

The following do not give a person a right standing before God. The following do not take away sins of man:

- Self-righteousness
- Social and political reforms
- Human intelligence
- Religions of this world
- Performance-based Christianity
- Pleasant and civilised environment
- The Law — The Ten Commandments or the Old Covenant

It is only Jesus Christ and his finished work that can take away sins of man and give the person a right standing before God.

In the Bible, we read about a Jewish religious group called the Pharisees. These people never really benefited from the coming of Jesus, all because of their self-righteousness. Sadly, in our world today, we have people who believe self-righteousness gives them a right standing before God. This is performance-based Christianity or salvation by works and sustained by works. This is an insult to Jesus Christ as Hebrews 10:29 says.

Performance-based Christianity tells us that the finished work of Jesus Christ is not enough to give a person a right standing before God. It leads people to doing or adding something to the finished work — like putting on a church uniform or giving a lot to a charity, thinking this will give one a right standing before God. When this happens, Grace ceases to be Grace, and, like the Pharisees, this person will not benefit from the amazing grace of God. As mentioned above, trying to improve on Jesus' finished work is an insult to Christ.

In 2 Kings 4:38-41, we see a story of a person trying to improve using human effort, the work of Grace (Elisha).

What was the result of human effort being added to the work of Grace (Jesus' finished work)? Death in the pot!

The finished work of Jesus Christ qualifies us to receive spiritual gifts, which, when properly used, enable those with these gifts to become a blessing to others and to the body of Christ. Ephesians 4:11-12 says, *"It was he who gave some to be apostles, some to be prophets, some to be evangelists, and some to be pastors and teachers to prepare God's people for works of service so that the body of Christ may be built up."*

Note that these spiritual gifts are not there to make people into church administrators but to thoroughly feed God's sheep on the Gospel of God's grace, so that those who are fed will go on to feed other believers, thus starting a chain reaction. If this could be done, the evangelism of a greater portion of the world could be quickly accomplished.

We believe in Jesus Christ because He is God and because God said we should believe in Him. He is the only source of eternal salvation; He is the only way for us to live lives that glorify God.

We believe in Jesus Christ because only through Him are we made alive (Ephesians 2:1-22). We believe in Jesus because of His unsearchable riches (Ephesians 3:8). We believe in Jesus because He is the fullness of God; He is the fulfilment of the whole Law; He is the Light of the World, the Bread of Life; He is the Way, the Truth, and the Life (John 14:6). We believe in Jesus Christ because of His great superiority in His person and His work (Hebrews Chapters 1-10) — the giver and the gift are very superior).

Jesus is the only solution to all our personal problems and the problems of the whole world. Jesus Christ is the only solution to the world's deepest problem — the sinful nature of man.

Faith in Jesus is high regard for God, and unbelief is high regard of one- self. If we do not believe in the Son of God, we will be saying God is a liar (1 John 5:10). I believe in the Son of God because I know God is not a liar. I believe in the Son of God because it is only He who can make me walk in the truth of the Gospel.

CHAPTER 3

From Religion to Christianity

One of the major things that our Lord Jesus came to do in the world was to establish a class of people that had never existed before in the world, called Christians, the church, new creation, new man (Ephesians 2:14-16). The church was established in a world where people already had their own religions. Some people, such as the Jews, already had Judaism as their religion. The Law of Moses was their rule of life. The Law was and is still made up of things like the Ten Commandments, various offerings and festivals, the tabernacle and various furniture items in it, the priest, and his priestly garments. Major aspects of the Law were strict instructions, rules and regulations to be followed, and failure to obey just one resulted in punishment. The religion of the Jews was not manmade — it was given to them by God.

All other groups of non-Jewish people in the world at that time were the Gentiles. What was their rule of life? How did they know right from wrong? Romans 2:14-15 gives us an idea of how the Gentiles lived. The Bible tells us that the nature of man, or man's Conscience, as created by God, was originally good, knowing right from wrong, perfectly corresponding with God and His law. So for the Gentiles, man's conscience was the rule of life. But as time went by, people moved away from God's law and started to worship idols, just as is seen in the world today. This shows the weakness of 'religion'. Religion does not empower people to do the right thing. Religion places emphasis on the person doing for his or her God. In religion, there is punishment for failing to obey; blessings come as a result of works. In religion, the person is the centre of everything, and everything depends on the person. The best that religion can do for the person is to reform him or her, but it cannot regenerate a person. Regeneration is being born again in the spirit, to form a new creation.

In Christianity, Jesus is the centre of everything. Christianity is all about Christ, and its fulfillment depends on Him and Him alone. Jesus came into the world to die for sinners so that all who believe in Him are forgiven of their sins, receive eternal life and become children of God. In Christianity, the emphasis is on God doing for the believer (Hebrews 8: 10-12), and Christ is the rule of life in Christianity.

The believer is regenerated, born again (John 3:3). In Christianity, Christ finished all the work, and all that the person has to do to be blessed is to believe in Jesus Christ and receive from Him what he has accomplished for the believer. In Christianity, blessings do not come by works but by right believing — believing in Jesus Christ and his finished work. Does this not promote laziness? No — when people are saved, they are also empowered to do Godly works (Ephesians 2:10). Look at the apostle Paul and what he was able to do from the moment he was converted to Christianity. Would you call him a lazy person? No, not at all, and yet he totally depended on the grace of God.

The other major difference between religion and Christianity is that, in religion, people do or don't do something because it is considered right or wrong by the society in which one lives. In Christianity, the consideration for doing or not doing is whether Christ is leading or the self is leading. Is it spirit or self and not right or wrong.? Right or wrong as the basis for doing or not doing something is the teaching of religion and not Christianity. See *Basic Elements of the Christian Faith*, by Witness Lee. In religion, the mind is always controlled by the flesh, while in Christianity, the spirit is supposed to take the upper hand in controlling the mind. Religion is based on people's culture and traditional beliefs. Christianity has nothing to do with peoples' culture or traditional beliefs. It is all about Christ. The Apostle Paul had to say goodbye to his culture, his traditions, and his religion to gain Christ (to be a Christian) (Philippians 3:7-9).

If culture were important for one to be a Christian, Paul would not have abandoned it, especially when you consider that, by saying goodbye to his own culture, he became a real enemy of his own people, who had not yet accepted Jesus Christ.

Conversion to Christianity

The word 'salvation' comes from the Greek word *sozo*, meaning 'wholeness of the body', 'saved', 'healed', 'delivered', 'joy', 'peace'.

Salvation is a spiritual process that takes place inside — out of a believer. It starts in the spirit of a person. A person is made up of three distinct parts, and these are spirit, soul and body (1 Thessalonians 5:23), as shown in the diagram below.

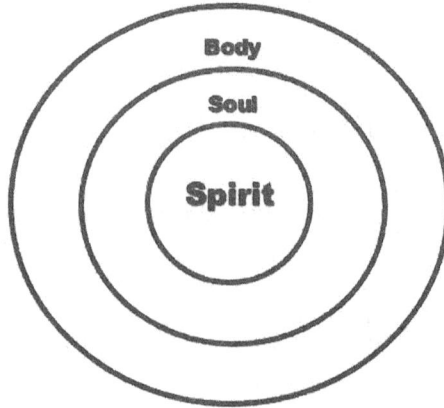

THE THREE PARTS
OF A PERSON

Diagrams from basic elements of Christian faith ...

As shown in the diagram, the spirit is the innermost part of a person. This is where Christ comes to live in a believer, and this is the part that enables us to contact God (John 4:24; Romans 1:9). This is the **Spiritual realm**. The soul is the part that deals with our thoughts, decisions, desires and emotions. This is our very self, our personality (Matthew 16:26; Luke 9:25. This is the **Psychological realm**. The body is our external part; it deals with the material world. This is the **Physical realm**.

SIN ENTERED MAN.
AND THE HOLY
GOD COULD NOT
COME INTO AN
UNHOLY PERSON

At the cross, our Lord Jesus Christ accomplished all that is required for a person to be forgiven for his or her sins and be clothed by God's righteousness (to be saved and become a child of God). The finished work of our Lord Jesus Christ on the cross fully satisfied God's requirements for our salvation, and there is no other way that a person can be forgiven of his sins and receive God's righteousness.

The Major Steps in the Process of Salvation (*sozo*)

- God calls people to the preaching ministry
- God anoints preachers with His spirit and power. For service, this enables them to say words with power to convict people of sin
- The preachers are sent by God to preach the Gospel of Jesus Christ, the Good News.
- What is this 'Good News'? It is about God's amazing love, love that made Him to leave heaven and come as a person (incarnation) into the world and live in this world as a person called Jesus Christ. He came to die a painful and shameful death, and His resurrection qualified all who believe in Jesus to receive forgiveness of sin and God's gift of righteousness and eternal life.
- The Gospel of Grace teaches people and makes people to know who Jesus Christ is: His birth and death, the cross, that he is the Lamb of God, Lord and Saviour. By believing in Him, one receives forgiveness, grace, justification (Romans 3:23-26), the Holy Spirit, the gift of no condemnation, and the gift of righteous salvation. This will help people believe the one they know (Romans 10:14-15). Does this mean that people should not preach from the Old Testament? This question continues to come up. As I have said before in this book, preachers must preach from every part of the Bible but must emphasise making believers see Jesus in the Scriptures (Old Testament included).

See Luke 24: 25-27; Acts 10: 4.

- An example of seeing Jesus in the scriptures is to look at Boaz the kinsman redeemer in Ruth 4:14 as a picture of Jesus. Look at Joseph (Genesis 50:19-21) forgiving his brothers as a picture of Jesus. When we look at the Bible more closely, we see that the greater part of the Old Testament is Jesus Christ concealed, or Jesus Christ as shadows and that the New Testament is Jesus Christ revealed.

- When people are hearing anointed preaching of the gospel of Jesus Christ, the spirit of God moves into people's hearts, convicting them of sin, revealing sin, and showing the need for a saviour. A good example of this is what happened when Jonah (Jonah 3:4-5) spoke to the people of Nineveh the very words given to him by God. What was the result? *Every Day with Jesus*/ 15 August 2015 says, 'because it was a message that carried with it the convicting power of God's Holy Spirit, all that Jonah was requested to do was speak the words. God's spirit then took over and applied the message to the hearts of the people'.

- What is the result of the work of the Holy Spirit on people's hearts? The Holy Spirit makes people to believe in Jesus Christ, accepting Jesus as Lord and Saviour. Divine exchange takes place; see diagram below.

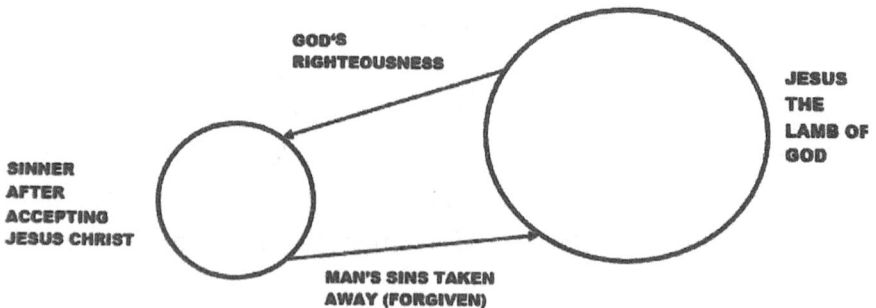

GOD'S RIGHTEOUSNESS

JESUS THE LAMB OF GOD

SINNER AFTER ACCEPTING JESUS CHRIST

MAN'S SINS TAKEN AWAY (FORGIVEN)

See Romans 10:9-13, John 1:12-13, and Ephesians 2:8-10.

The above readings show clearly that salvation is by grace through faith and not by works. Good works are a result of being saved (fruit of the spirit).

Faith > salvation > good works.

Unfortunately, some people today, mostly because of their great desire to be independent, believe in salvation by works, doings things like:

- keeping the Ten Commandments
- giving to charity
- living a moral and respectable life
- church attendance

All this is wrong believing and does not lead to salvation. Self-righteousness takes a person away from God, just like the Pharisees we read about in the Bible.

• The spirit of God now joins with the spirit of man impacting divine life onto the spirit of man. This makes the spirit of man, which was dead because of sin, come alive. The spirit of man, which is now alive, occupied, and energised by the spirit of God, is now supposed to take over the rule and control of the human soul and body. This is God's original plan. This makes a believer to be a "spiritual man" (1 Corinthians 2:15). This is the process of regeneration, being born again. So the part of the person that is born again is the spirit. John 3:6 says, *"flesh gives birth to flesh, but the spirit gives birth to spirit!"*

Body

Soul

Spirit

GOD'S LIFE
HAS COME IN

→ **REGENERATED
BORN AGAIN**

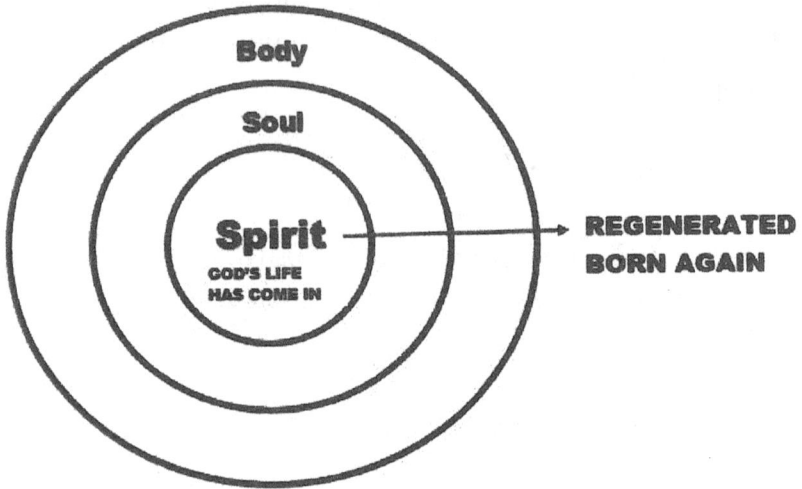

The believer can now be baptized to show that he/she identifies himself/herself with Christ. Showing faith in Christ involves identifying oneself with His death, burial, and resurrection. Baptism (being immersed into water — from the Greek word *baptizo*): Is it scriptural to baptize infants? Baptism is for believers only — those who have accepted Jesus Christ as their personal Lord and Saviour.

- After regeneration, the process of transformation of the soul begins. God's life in the spirit of the believer begins to spread from the believer's Spirit into the believer's soul (Romans 12:2; 2 Corinthians 3:18), such that one's thoughts, desires, and decisions begin to show Christ-likeness. This is a lifelong process.

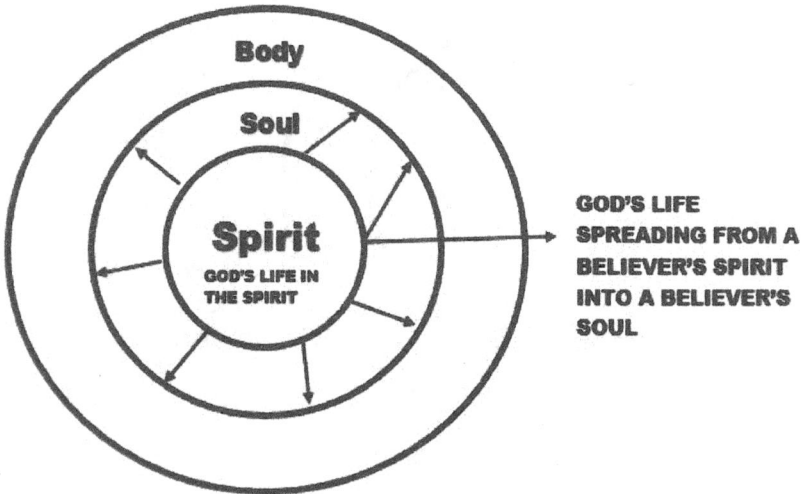

At this stage, the spirit has been sanctified by this process of regeneration and now the soul is being sanctified as the life-giving spirit, spread from the spirit to the soul of the believer (Romans 12:2; 2 Corinthians 3:18). The body remains unredeemed until the Second Coming of Jesus Christ. This explains the problems we experience with our flesh, such as death, pain, sin, lust, and hunger.

- At the Second Coming of Jesus, God's life spreads into the body, transfiguring our bodies by His life power. The transfiguration of our bodies is called glorification (Philippians 3:21).

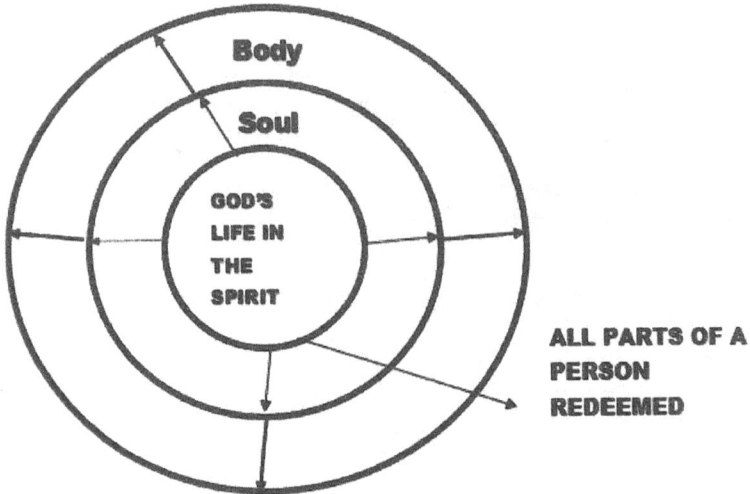

When this happens, God's plan of salvation is then complete.

Note: Sanctification is the process of setting apart the believer to God from the world, from sin and from self.

Signs of Salvation
- Showing a desire for the things of God, obeying God, doing God's will (Acts 16:6)
- Desiring to pray (Acts 2:42)
- Showing true love to all people — believers and nonbelievers — including one's enemies
- Showing desire to fellowship with other believers (Acts 2:42)

Why Does God Call Us?
To become a Christian is a calling from God. God does this so that Christ can come and live in those called Christians. They will have accepted Jesus Christ as Lord and Saviour (Colossians 1:27; Galatians 2:20). Christ in the believer begins the process of transformation so

that Christ-like characteristics are expressed in the world through believers, as we see in life of the Apostle Paul.

The Apostle Paul

"...but whatever were gains to me I now consider loss for the sake of Christ. What is more, I consider everything a loss because of the surpassing worth of knowing Christ Jesus my Lord, for whose sake I have lost all things. I consider them rubbish that I may gain Christ and be found in him, not having a righteousness of my own that comes from the law..." (Philippians 3:7-9).

The title of this book, *From Religion to Christianity*, comes from the passage quoted above. This is a Bible passage from one of the books written by Paul. In this passage, Paul is showing us things he had to say goodbye to in his life for him to gain Christ, for him to be transformed from religion (Judaism) to Christianity, for him to be transformed from Law to Grace, for him to be transformed from the Old Covenant to the New Covenant.

The first time we meet Paul in the Bible is in Acts 8:1; at that time, he was called 'Saul', not 'Paul'. At that time, he was well known for working very zealously to destroy the church. To him, Christianity was a great threat to his culture and his traditional beliefs, to the Law of Moses and to his religion, Judaism. Then we meet him in Chapter 9 of the book of Acts. Salvation came to him while he was on the way to Damascus to arrest any Christian he found there (Acts 9:1-5).

His encounter with Jesus on the road to Damascus resulted in his conversion from his religion, Judaism, to Christianity, and his zeal and determination to destroy the church was turned by God into zeal and determination to build the church. The conversion of Paul from Judaism to Christianity did not please most Jews, who now saw him as a traitor or a rebel — the way Paul used to look at Christians. Now it was he who was being persecuted for being a Christian.

The following Biblical quotation shows the nature of the challenges that Paul faced by boldly proclaiming the Gospel of Grace. *"...the next morning the Jews formed a conspiracy and bond themselves with an oath not to eat or drink until they had killed Paul"* (Acts 23:12). In Acts 14:19, some Jews beat him very severely and dragged him out of the city, thinking he was dead.

Paul was a rebel with a cause. The cause was for him to gain Christ so that he could show others how they could also be saved (the Gospel). Paul's other desire was to help others walk in the truth of the Gospel, to build up God's people (the church). From this, we can say that Paul's — ministry can be summarized in two words: The Gospel and the church. See Ephesians 3:8-9.

The table below shows things that Paul said goodbye to in order to gain salvation.

Religious Things That Paul Said Goodbye to for His Salvation	What Paul Gained When Saved
• Circumcision (Galatians 6:15) • Keeping the Sabbath (Colossians 2:16-17) • Not Eating Certain Foods (1 Timothy 4:3-5) • Self-Righteousness (Philippians 3:9) • Feasts and Offerings (Colossians 2:16-17) • The Law of Moses and Judaism (The Old Covenant) • Shadows or Pictures	Christ
Old Truth	New Truth

In Paul, God is showing what Christ can do when He lives in a person. In Paul, God is showing a true example of a person who was transformed and transferred from religion (Judaism) to Christianity. Paul said goodbye to everything in religion as he was being made into a Christian.

This is the reason why Christ came, why he died, and why he was resurrected: So that those who believe in Jesus will be transferred from religion to Christianity and to show the seriousness of our salvation — it cost God the death of His beloved Son. When God created the world and all that is in it, he just spoke a word *"Let there be light and there was light"* (Genesis 1:3). There was no shedding of blood involved in that big task of creation, but when it came to our salvation, there was need for blood. Does the world take the issue of sin as seriously as God does? You and I — do we take the issue of sin as seriously as God does?

Contextualisation and Syncretism

Some things that have greatly diluted the gospel today are contextualisation and syncretism.

- Contextualisation, in theology, is an attempt to present Christianity in a culturally relevant way. An example would be Ed Stetzer's book *Comeback Churches*. Is this in agreement with the message of the Cross? No — not at all. The message of the Cross is the very opposite of human culture, human wisdom, and human intelligence (1 Corinthians 1:18-25). *Believer's Bible Commentary*, by William MacDonald, says 'Efforts to make the Gospel more acceptable are completely misguided. There is a vast difference between God's wisdom and man's, and there is no use trying to reconcile them'.

- From the above statement, we see that contextualising Christianity is a scripturally incorrect approach. Christianity is all about Christ, Christ living in a believer, Christ expressing himself in and through a believer. In trying to make Christianity relevant to culture, cultural things end up being looked upon as part of the Christian faith. There is a great danger of human improvising/ human effort being made part of Christianity. There is a great danger, in that Christ's finished work will be looked upon as being insufficient in satisfying God's requirements for our salvation. This is a real insult to Christ. In Hebrews 10:29, the Bible has a warning for people who treat Christ in such a manner. So, is there room for contextualisation in Christianity?

- No, not at all. Did our Lord Jesus attempt to present the Gospel in a cultural relevant way? The answer is 'No'. Our Lord Jesus greatly violated some Jewish cultural and religious practices. Jesus healed on a Sabbath; Jesus talked to woman in a public place, and the woman was a Samaritan (John 4:7). This was very contrary to the Jewish culture. Jesus' inner circle was made up of 12 male disciples and a number of women. One of them, Mary Magdalene, became a follower of Jesus. Jesus actually greatly raised the status of women to be equal with men in Jewish society. Again, this was very contrary to the Jewish culture. Did Paul attempt to present the Gospel in a way relevant to culture?

- The answer is 'No — not at all'. In Colossians 2:8, Paul says, *"See to it that no-one takes you captive through hollow and deceptive philosophy, which depends on human tradition and the basic principles of this world rather than on Christ."* In this passage, he is saying, 'No' to bringing human traditions into Christianity. Paul actually said goodbye to his cultural practices to gain Christ (Philippians 3:8). Because of this, Jews who were non-believers (and these were the majority) looked at Paul as a traitor, a real enemy of Judaism.

• Syncretism is amalgamation of two or more religious belief systems. The *Oxford Advanced Learners Dictionary* defines it as involving, adapting, and adopting some aspects from this and that religion to form a new religion.

In some modern secular societies, blending of religions is done to reduce inter-religion tension, but this is scripturally incorrect. Did Paul try to mix Judaism and Christianity? No, not at all. As pointed out above, in Philippians 3:8 Paul said goodbye to every aspect of Judaism.

When he became a Christian, what did he say about circumcision? Galatians 6:15 saus, *"Neither circumcision nor non-circumcision means anything"*. What did he say about the Sabbath? He said it's a shadow of things that were to come (Colossians 2:16-17). Is there room for syncretism in Christianity?

The answer is 'No, not at all'. We see in the Old Testament that the Jewish kings and priests who were considered evil were those who mixed Judaism with other foreign religious practices. In other words, they were guilty of contextualisation and syncretism. All Jewish kings and priests who upheld Judaism simply as Judaism — with no human improvising — were considered by God to be good kings and good priests. Look at 2 Chronicles 14:1-15: Asa, king of Judah, when he came to power, starts by removing anything that belonged to foreign gods, and he commanded Judah to obey God's Law. He became a successful king, but in the last years of his reign, Asa started to rely on human effort and not God (2 Chronicles 16:7-9). The result of this was that peace departed from Asa. Also see 1 Kings 16:29-34 for an evil king who worshipped Baal.

Take a look at Daniel 1:8. We see Daniel, a Jew, in Babylon, refusing to eat food not in keeping with Judaism. Daniel shows us that mixing God's ways with human ways never pleases God.

So if there was no room for human improvising in Judaism (a religion) and everything was to be done according to the instructions given to Moses on the mount by God, it follows that there is no room for human effort or human works in Christianity. The Bible, in Romans 12:2 makes it very clear what believers need to do in relation to the world, culture, and customs: The believers belong to the kingdom of God — and not to the world.

The world has cultures and customs very different from those of the kingdom of God. Christ came to deliver us from the world into the kingdom of God. Believers are to take the Gospel into the world for the salvation of mankind, so that the people will be delivered from the world — not for believers to be transformed by the world.

In view of this, will it not be looked upon a willful sin for believers to attempt to relate Christianity to cultures of the world, and will it not be a willful sin to amalgamate Christianity with other religions and other cultures? Christianity is all about Christ. Even the faith we have is a gift from God (Romans 12:3). It is very sad to note that, today, some Christians have taken some aspects of Judaism and blended them into Christian belief. Examples of some things from Judaism that have been brought into Christianity are: a humanly ordained priesthood, Aaronic priestly garments, Sabbath- keeping, holy places, holy water, candles, and some feasts and festivals.

This is syncretism and contextualisation; Christianity can never be

Christianity if such things are done. There is a warning in the word of God about such practices, willfully departing from the Gospel of Grace as stated in the Bible, in Hebrews 10:29: *"How more severely do you think a man deserves to be punished who has trampled the Son of God under foot, who has treated as an unholy thing the blood of the covenant that sanctified and who has insulted the spirit of grace?"* Apostle Paul raises similar concerns with the Galatians (Galatians 4:8-20).

So contextualisation and syncretism are an insult to Christ. Grace is weakened when mixed with the Law or human effort. Does this not explain why today some Christians have no impact on other people's lives and their own lifestyles are not different from those of non-believers? Does this not also explain why some church assemblies are getting smaller and smaller?

Today, God's desire is for all people to become believers — to have Christ born in us, to have Christ live in us, and to have Christ formed in us. When this happens, a person is said to have been *transformed and transferred* by the Holy Spirit and divine life from:

- Shadows to substance
- Ritual to reality
- Judaism to Christ
- The Old Covenant to the New Covenant
- Law to grace
- Religion to Christianity
- Old Truth to New Truth
- From the spirit of world to the spirit of God

Old Truth and New Truth

What is the Old Truth, and what is the New Truth? The Law is the Old Truth. It was the rule of life at a certain time and to a particular group of people, but, today, it is no longer the truth, and it is no longer the rule of life or rule of worship for believers. Grace (Christ) is the New Truth. It is the rule of life, and it is the rule of worship for believers today (Hebrews 10:1 and Colossians 2:16-17).

Hebrews 8:13 says, *"By calling this covenant new, he has made the first obsolete, and what is obsolete and edging will soon disappear"*. The Old Covenant, or the Law, is what is being referred to as obsolete in the passage above. This is the Old Truth. But today, Christ (New Truth) has appeared, so the Old Truth has to disappear.

Question? Why do we have Christians today who are still clinging to what the Bible calls 'obsolete'? Our lord came, died, and was resurrected so as to transfer all who believe in him from Old Truth to New Truth.

Old Truth	New Truth
Law (Hebrews 8:13)	Grace (Hebrews 8:13)
Sabbath-keeping a must for all Jews (Exodus 31:13)	Sabbath-keeping irrelevant to all believers (Colossians 2:16-17)
Circumcision a must for all male Jews (Genesis 17:10)	Circumcision not scripturally relevant (Galatians 6:15)
Clean food and unclean food (Leviticus Chapter 11)	All food clean for eating (1 Timothy 4:2-5; Colossians 2:16-19)
Eye for an eye (Exodus 21:24). Stripe for stripe.	By his wounds you are healed (1 Peter 2:24)
Give to be given (Luke 6:38)	Give cheerfully. God's grace continuously supplies your needs (2 Corinthians 9:7-8)
Forgive to be forgiven (Matthew 6:14)	Forgive because the Lord has forgiven you at Calvary (Colossians 3:13 and Ephesians 4:32)

Our Lord Jesus came to deliver us from Old Truth to New Truth. Moving from Old Truth to New Truth is really being in step with God.

CHAPTER 4

Building Up God's People

Who are God's people? In this book, 'God's people' refers to the church: Saints, new creation, new man, and Christians, and building up of God's people is the process of spiritual growth of a believer. It is a lifelong process that starts at the conversion of a person. The major players in the spiritual growth of a person are church meetings such as church services, Bible study, prayer meetings (individual and group Bible studies and prayer meetings), fellowship groups, preachers, other believers, and any other church activities, including mission work.

Church meetings are very important in that, through them, believers communicate with God and interact with other believers. This is the time believers are fed on that which brings about a spiritual growth, so it is a big challenge to those who organise and conduct these church meetings to make sure they are exposing believers to material which enables them to walk in the truth of the Gospel. Through church meetings, believers are strengthened, supported, and encouraged to remain faithful and to be on guard — to be alert and to keep watch as our Lord Jesus commanded (Mark 13:33-37), to keep in step with God.

What Really Brings About Spiritual Growth?

The Apostle Paul gives us the answer to this question. *"Now I commit you to God and to the word of his grace which is able to build you up and give you an inheritance among all those who are sanctified"* (Acts 20: 32).

Two things stand out very clearly in this Bible passage:

1. People are built up by the Gospel of Grace. What is the Gospel of Grace? This is the Good News about our Lord, Jesus Christ and God's amazing love, God's favour/grace to us sinners. We deserve death, but because of His love, the Son of God came from heaven to die a very painful death on the cross so that those who believe in Him might receive forgiveness of sins, everlasting life, God's righteousness, God's grace, and the spirit of God so that they become children of God.

   So the Gospel of Grace is God's power for salvation to all who believe (Romans 1:16). It breaks the power of sin in and over the believer. The Gospel of God is the power and life of God that transform a believer into a new man or new creation, the church. It is the power of God that transforms a person from living under the Law to living under Grace.

2. The above Bible passage also shows very clearly that it is not a person or human effort that builds up good people. If this were so, Paul would have said so, but he just talked about the word of his Grace, which is able to build up God's people. Paul said these words in his farewell remarks to the Ephesian church elders. Paul

repeats the same message of building up God's people in Titus 2:11-12. "*... For the grace of God that brings salvation has appeared to all men. It teaches us to say no to ungodliness and worldly passions and to live self-controlled, upright, and godly lives in this present age*".

Again, we see that the building up of God's people is done by the Gospel of Jesus Christ. The above Bible passages clearly show that the process of building up God's people is a spiritual matter and not of human effort or human wisdom. As stated at the opening of this chapter, God's people are the church. The church is people or a person who has accepted Jesus Christ as Lord and Saviour and Christ now dwells in that person. Both Jews and Gentile believers formed the church.

How did the church start, what makes it grow, how is it sustained, and why was it formed?

The Tabernacle

To be able to answer the above questions, we need to start by reading Exodus 31:1-11. In this passage, Moses is being given instructions by God on how to build the Tabernacle and what was to be in it, e.g., the Ark of the Covenant, the altar of burnt offerings, and several other items, including priestly garments. Moses was also given instructions on who was to do the work. In Exodus 31:2-11, God says to Moses, "See, I've chosen Bezalel's son Uri, son of Uhur, of the tribe of Judah, and I have filled him with the spirit of God, with the skill and ability and knowledge in all kinds of crafts to make artistic designs..." They were to make the Tabernacle just as the Lord had commanded.

Let us now take a closer look at the Tabernacle.

The building of the Tabernacle and its use are very similar to the process of building up God's people and their use in the world. When the Law was given to the children of Israel, one of the most important things they were instructed to build by God was the Tabernacle. The Tabernacle was God's earthly dwelling place, and it was used as a place of worship. The tabernacle was a tent-like structure. God gave specific instructions as to how it was to be built, the materials to be used, the dimensions of the Tabernacle, the shape, divisions in it, the furniture to go in it, and their specific position in the Tabernacle. God also called and equipped men with skills required for putting up the Tabernacle: Craftsman, designer and embroiderer — these were skills given to Bezalel and Oholiab by God Himself for the building of the Tabernacle (Exodus 38:21-31 and Exodus 31:1-11).

The furniture that was to be in the tabernacle was as follows:

The Ark of the Covenant, in the most holy place; altar of incense, table of showbread, and the golden lamp stand. In the holy place, a bronze laver and altar of burnt offering; these were in the outer court. The Most Holy Place and the Holy Place were separated by a veil made of fine woven linen.

No human wisdom or intelligence was needed in the construction of the Tabernacle or in anything that took place in the Tabernacle. *Believers Bible Commentary*, by William MacDonald, page 118, has something to say about this: "The great single requirement in making these objects was to follow the pattern which God gave on the mountain, and there was no room for human improvising. So it is with spiritual matters: We must follow divine direction and not deviate from the pattern that the Lord in his wisdom has given." So if clear instructions were given to build a Tabernacle, God's temporary earthly dwelling place during the old Testament Times, it follows that [there should be clear instructions] to build up God's people ('the church'), who are God's permanent earthly dwelling place.

The Bible, which is God's instructions, must be strictly adhered to. Just as in the case of the Tabernacle, all involved in the building up of God's people must be the people called and equipped by God with His Gospel of Grace. As we saw above, it is God's Grace that builds up God's people.

Spiritual Growth

The Gospel of our Lord Jesus Christ gives clear instructions on how a person becomes a child of God, a Christian, and how a believer is sustained and grows to become a mature Christian.

Everything about spiritual growth and spiritual life is the work of the Holy Spirit, Who dwells in the believer.

Preachers are empowered, equipped, and sent out to preach the Gospel of Grace by the Holy Spirit. The Gospel of Grace is about Jesus Christ coming into the world to die for sinners. His death on the Cross, known as the 'finished work', satisfied God's requirements for the forgiveness of sin and for man to receive the righteousness of God. The Gospel of Grace teaches that Christ is God and that Christianity is all about Christ — not human effort. Christianity is all about the Grace of God, just as in the birth of Isaac, who was born when both Abraham and Sarah were well beyond childbearing age (Romans 4:18-21). The Gospel of Grace teaches people that a person is justified by Grace through faith in Jesus and not by human works.

A believer is forgiven his past, present, and future sins and, once forgiven, there is no more room for condemnation in that person because he/she will be in Christ. It teaches that Jesus is the conquering Christ, who is also the Light of the World and Saviour of all mankind.

A good detailed and accurate knowledge of Jesus Christ and his finished work and also what finished work has really accomplished for a believer all give a very strong Christian foundation. Such a good foundation equips the believer to resist the devil and false teachers. This knowledge equips the believer with tools to endure challenges that Christians face in their day-to-day lives. So anointed preaching — which is preaching that comes from preachers called and equipped by God, preachers full of the grace and spirit of God, preachers with the gift of prophecy which enables them to speak the Word of God with authority and power — makes the spirit of God move into people hearts, convicting them of sin and leading them to accepting Jesus as Lord and Saviour.

The spirit of God, also known as the life-giving spirit, imparts divine life to the believer's spirit. This makes the spirit of the believer come alive and join with the spirit of God, taking over its role, which is to rule and control the whole mind, which leads to the control of the whole person. A person who is ruled and controlled by his spirit is a spiritual man (1 Corinthians 1:12-15).

When this happens, a believer is said to be born again (regeneration) in his/her spirit by the Holy Spirit (redemption of the spirit). Christ (the spirit of God) now comes to dwell in the believers, making you the believer to be part of the body of Christ (1 Corinthians 12:13). This is **baptism** of the holy spirit; empowering the believer for worship and Service (John 14: 16) this is the result of the believer being **indwelt** by the Holy Spirit and teaching the believer things of God (1 John 2:27). This is due to the **anointing** of the Holy Spirit.

The next stage is now the spreading of divine life from the spirit into the soul.

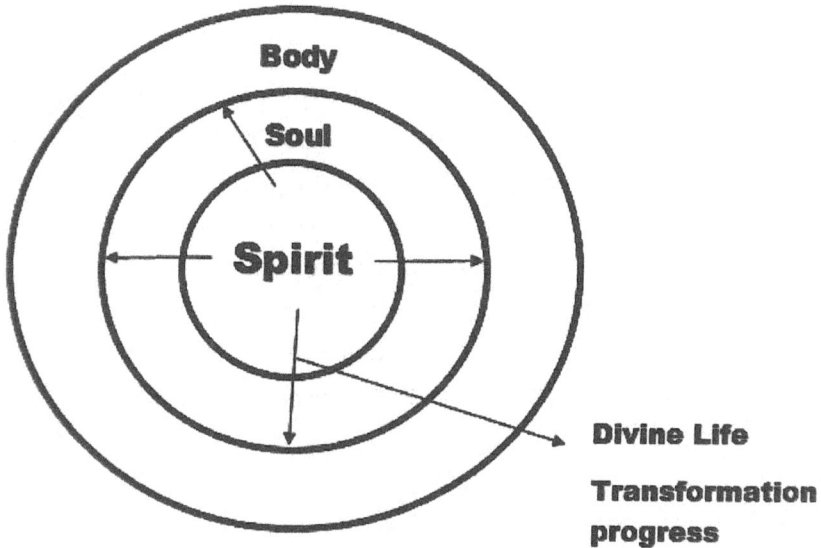

The soul is transformed, resulting in Christ-like characteristics, which will start to be shown by the believer. This is a lifelong process. This is the redemption of the soul. As the believer continues to be fed on the Gospel of Grace, by anointed preachers and preachers with the gift of prophecy, more and more Christ-like characteristics develop in the believer. Paul, in Galatians 4:19, describes this as Christ having being formed in a believer. This is God's greatest desire in every believer.

NOTE: From all this, we see that if people are fed on the Old Truth (the Law), there is no spiritual growth. But if people are fed on the New Truth we see spiritual growth.

The Gift of Prophecy

"Follow the way of love and eagerly desire spiritual gifts, especially the gift of prophecy" (1 Corinthians 14:1).

Why does Paul say this? It is because prophecy edifies and builds the church. To prophesy is to speak for the Lord and speak forth the Lord. Prophecy is ministering Christ to the people with authority and boldness, and in a language well understood by the people; ministering Christ to the people is the main reason for church services, Bible study, prayer meetings, and all other church meetings. The result of ministering Christ to the people is edification, which is spiritual growth. The Bible says, *"… try to excel in gifts that build up the Church"* (1 Corinthians 14:12).

What happens in spiritual growth is that the believer grows in faith and becomes more and more Christ-like, showing that Christ is being formed in the believer. So when the Gospel of Grace is preached with boldness and authority, conversion of sinners takes place, baby Christians are transformed into mature Christians, and mature Christians show that Christ has been formed in a believer! This is the *building up* of God's people.

Why the Church Was Formed

- To form a class of people who are reconciled to God and live a life that gives glory to Christ (Ephesians 2:14-16; Ephesians 3:21). This formed a class of people who could approach God at any time. Before the church was formed, the Jews could approach God only once a year, on the Day of Atonement, and it was only the high priest who was allowed into the Holy of Holies, where the presence of God was. The Gentiles had no access to the true God.

- To form a class of people who would proclaim the gospel of grace worldwide (mission work) (Acts 1:8)
- To form a class of people who respond to the needs and welfare of other people worldwide (mission work) (Romans 12:9-21; Titus 3:1-8)
- To form a class of people who are neither Jews nor Gentiles — to reduce human hostility, e.g., **anti-Semitism** (Ephesians 2:14-16). This was God's way of reconciling a human to other human beings.
- For the Gentiles to have the same, equal rights and privileges as the Jews. Ephesians 3:6 says, *"This mystery, is that through the Gospel, the Gentiles are heirs together with Israel, members together of one body and share together in the promise in Christ"* Colossians Ch 1:26-29 says the same thing.
- The formation of the church was also a way of freeing the Jews from the Law
- The church was also formed so that there is a class or body of people where Christ is the head and He can express Himself through that body.
- *The church was created to form God's dwelling place* (Ephesians 2:22).

NOTE: From all this, we can say the church is there for the glory of God and welfare of all people.

The Main Stages of Spiritual Growth

- Christ is being born in a believer at the time a person believes in Jesus Christ — being 'born again'.
- Christ lives in a believer during a believer's Christian life (Galatians 2:20) Divine life spreading into the soul-transformation.
- Christ is formed in a believer when what one believes matures to the point of having thoughts, decisions, and desires — being 'Christ-like' (Galatians 4:19)

Signs of Spiritual Growth

- Showing love to all believers and nonbelievers (1 Peter 2:17)
- Showing more openness of every aspect of one's life to Christ
- Showing a more-prayerful life. Spiritual things take precedence over material things
- Showing more dependence and reliance on God in everything
- Being Christ conscious and not sin conscious (sin was dealt with by Christ at Calvary)
- When one freely declares, 'I am the righteousness of God in Christ' (2 Corinthians 5:21)
- Declaring 'I have the gift of no condemnation. Jesus was condemned on the Cross on our behalf (Romans 8:1)
- Living a life that glorifies Christ and not the self
- Showing a desire to lead others to Christ and showing a desire to teach others the Gospel of Grace (Hebrews 5:12)
- Living a life in which right or wrong are not the major consideration for doing or not doing something but living a life led by Christ (Spirit), or the spiritual self are the major considerations for doing or not doing something; living in the spirit is the major sign of spiritual growth. This will also show that Christ has been

formed in the believer, which is God's greatest desire for the believer, and when Christ has been formed in the believer, the believer can then walk in the truth of the Gospel. That is a sign of real spiritual growth.

- Being Christ-like is the surest sign of spiritual growth.

CHAPTER 5

Challenges That Christians Face

'Every true child of God soon learns that the Christian life is warfare. The hosts of Satan are committed to hindering and obstructing the work of Christ and to knocking the individual soldier out of combat. The more effective a believer is for the Lord, the more he/she will experience the savage attacks of the enemy: the devil does not waste his ammunition on nominal Christians'.

— *Believer's Bible Commentary*
Page 1951
William MacDonald

The above quotation shows that the Christian life is a struggle against evil forces which operate in the heavenly realms and in this world, such as the flesh, the devil, and the world itself (Ephesians 6:12-18).

While this is true, our loving heavenly Father has also made available to us His Grace in abundance. Romans 5:20 tells us where challenges abound, Grace super-abounds. Ephesians 1:19-20 says God has made available to believers His mighty *Resurrection power*. This enables believers to endure challenges just as Christ did and also just as Paul did. We need to remember that today's Christians suffer because they are taking an active part in the production and building up of the church. So, this is God's way of equipping his servants. *This is wonderful news!* Believers today have at their disposal God's word and His Spirit to enable us to withstand and overcome the evil powers operating on us with the hope of making believers doubt, question, worry, fear, develop evil thoughts, become anxious, and much more.

Are You Really Saved?

What have you to show as proof that you are saved? This will be the question that The Evil One will ask the new believer.

New believers, in particular and some old believers do, from time to time, have this question come into their hearts. Causing a believer doubts about knowing that he or she is saved is one of the major weapons that The Evil One uses against the believer. This is a very strong weapon used by The Evil One. This weapon is meant to make the believer start to feel as though he/she has not been saved.

New believers should feel greatly encouraged by the fact that even our Lord Jesus faced a similar question from the devil. This was meant to make Him doubt. *"If you are the Son of God…"* (Matthew 3:3). Today, believers are still facing the same question from the devil: *'If you are saved, how come you have such health problems? How come you are facing so many challenges?*

Our Lord Jesus responded to the devil's question as follows: *'It is written...*' The believer also needs to respond to the devil using 1 John 5:13, which clearly says '*...it is written that those who believe in the Son of God know for sure that they are saved.*' The word of God in 1 John 5: 13 clearly says those who believe in Jesus are saved. John 1:12-13 and Romans 10: 9-13 help to clearly show how a person is saved. A person's salvation does not depend on one's feelings or one's thinking. It depends only on what the word of God says, and the word of God is the only thing that the believer must stand on for his/her salvation and use it to respond to the devil.

Believers — and new believers, in particular — need also to know that, once saved, one remains saved forever. John 10:28-30 tells us, 'Once saved, always saved.

While the word of God tells us from outside that we are saved, believers also have a witness inside, confirming salvation, and that is the Spirit of God inside a believer (Romans 8:16).

A believer's love for the other believers is also proof of salvation (1 John 3:14).

Believers also need to remind the devil that salvation was initiated by God and not by a person — and that, once saved, one is kept saved by God. John 15:16 says that a person is saved by Grace and sustained by Grace. It is also important to point out that God's love and grace are eternal and that one's salvation is based on such love and grace.

The Bible says that no sin, failure, or weakness on our part can separate us from the love of God, which is in Christ Jesus (Romans 8:35-39).

The believer's salvation is based also on God's righteousness (Psalm

89: 14). This makes our salvation very strong indeed. Our God is strong and never changes (John 10:28-29).

Another assurance and security of our salvation is the promise of Christ. He promised to keep us, to uphold us, and never leave us (John 6:37 and Hebrews 13:5).

The challenges discussed above show that what Christians struggle with are just spiritual problem, and these need a spiritual solution. One needs to continue looking up to Jesus and His 'finished work'. The finished work of Christ qualifies every believer to receive and use all that God has made available for fighting The Evil One.

The devil uses fear as a powerful tool that brings doubt. Even great men of God that we read about in the Bible have shown great fear or doubt in the course of their life. We read about David in the book of Samuel. He is a man who killed a lion and a bear while he was still a young man, while looking after his father's sheep. He showed total dependence on God in all this, and the Lord gave him victory over the champion of the Philistines, Goliath.

Even though God had given him so much victory, we meet him later on, showing so much fear. He said, *"One of these days I shall be destroyed by the hand of Saul; the best thing I can do is to escape to the land of the Philistines..."* (1 Samuel 27:1). In 1 Samuel 22:12, we read that *"David took these words to heart and was very much afraid of Achish, king of Gath. So he feigned insanity in their presence....."* Maybe, as God's anointed one, David did not want blood on his hands, so he chose to run away from Saul. Even when David got a chance to kill Saul, David spared Saul's life. But the Bible still tells us that David showed fear and ran away from Saul. With the king of Gath, David is said to have shown fear and pretended to be insane.

We see Prophet Elijah, a man who greatly depended on God, in 1 Kings 18:16-46 performing a great miracle on mount Carmel, and yet, in 1 Kings 19, we see Elijah running away from Jezebel, wife of King Ahab.

Today, we also experience moments of victory and other moments when we seem to show doubt and fear. Why does this happen even to those who are born again? At conversion, our spirit is redeemed, and, later, our soul is also redeemed, but our flesh is not redeemed until the Second Coming of Jesus, so the flesh, with its sinful nature, is still active in our lives and competing with the spirit to control the human mind (Galatians 5:17).

This is a challenge facing believers today. To overcome this problem, as said earlier on, God has made it possible for His Spirit to dwell in the believer, providing power to overcome the flesh. Such a believer is described as a spirit-led Christian, as opposed to the carnal/fleshly Christian, who is controlled by flesh and not by the spirit.

A large number of Christians today live a life that makes them no different from non-believers. Why? The reason most likely is that the believer has not grown from being carnal in nature.

Persecution

Christianity came into the world when there were already other religions, like Judaism. Those who belonged to Judaism saw a lot of good in it, but, more importantly, the Law came to them from God through Moses. So, to tell them to abandon Judaism for Christianity was very difficult for them. A number of Jews really resisted the change, and the result was that anybody who tried to promote Christianity was heavily persecuted. Persecution is one of the oldest problems that face Christians in this world. It can take a very violent nature, even in this so-called civilised world we live in today, and, at times, it can be non-violent, but it is still persecution.

Believer's Bible Commentary, by William MacDonald, page 2122, says 'A Godly life exposes the wickedness of others. People do not like to be thus exposed. Instead of repenting of their ungodliness and turning to Christ, they seek to destroy the one who has shown them up for what they really are'. Look at Mark 6:17-19. John the Baptist was beheaded for pointing out King Herod's sin.

From the above passages, we see that Christian persecution is spiritual warfare — the devil fighting God's people. True believers are aware of this, and, as a result, persecution has helped spread Christianity. In the Book of Acts, Chapter 8, the death of Steven and persecution of the church resulted in Christians being scattered. Thus, the Gospel spread, and the faith of believers grew.

Challenges do come to individual believers, but they also do come upon whole congregations, whole assemblies, or even upon the whole denomination. For example, when the church receives a government directive and is required to embrace something they consider sinful or unscriptural, the church is being asked to walk in a way or act in a way contrary to the truth of the Gospel.

The church can also feel challenged when it is constantly being asked to explain its relevance in this century.

In some Christian assemblies, their challenge is having very small congregations, with the majority of its members being the elderly. Such a congregation is not able to adequately support the various church programmes.

Here are some possible solutions to challenges that Christians face today:

- New believers need to be assisted to grow spiritually. See Acts 14:22. Paul spends a lot of time with new believers, helping them to grasp the real truth of the Gospel. Proper Bible study enables new believers to live according to the truth of the Gospel. This should be done by feeding them and teaching them the Gospel of Grace, which is the only thing that really empowers the believer to cope with the tricks of the devil, endure persecution, and resist the devil — especially in view of the fact that true believers know that the root cause of persecution is man's sinful nature (Christ overcame sin on our behalf 2000 years ago). Revenge or human effort does not deal with the root cause of the problem; revenge only worsens the situation. Since Christian life is warfare, the greatest need for every child of God is to have God's Grace and God's wisdom in abundance.

In this world, you can have everything, but without the grace of God, one has nothing in this world, because the devil will reign easily in that person's life (Romans 5:17). Christ's finished work qualified every believer to receive God's free supply of Grace, which empowers and supplies the believer with all his needs, enabling the believer to cope with even the worst persecution. Hebrews 12:15 shows the need for grace in abundance in all believer lives. It goes on to say, *"See to it that no-one misses the grace of God...."* Grace enables the believer to use the correct weapons in time of warfare — the correct weapons being *faith, prayer, and the word of God.*

Grace enables the believer to show love, kindness, goodness, and prayer for those who persecute. This is how Paul, in the book of Acts, reacted to persecution. The apostle Peter also gives a lot of encouragement to all those suffering for being Christians. Peter says our Lord Jesus was persecuted when He came into this world. So, believers, since they are Jesus' followers, cannot expect better treatment than was given to our Lord Jesus (1 Peter 4:12-19). Hebrews 12:5-11 shows that nothing happens by chance to a believer. God *allows* things to happen as part of transformation of the believer towards being Christ-like.

Apostasy

Apostasy is described in the Bible as an extraordinary, deliberate sin. Apostasy is when 'people hear the Gospel, make a profession of being Christians, become identified with a Christian church, and then abandon their profession of faith, decisively repudiate Christ, desert the Christian fellowship, and take their place with the enemies of the Lord Jesus Christ' (from *Believer's Bible Commentary*, by William MacDonald.

The above quotation explains in simple terms what Hebrews 6:4-6 says about this extraordinary sin. Please revisit that Bible passage.

Most sin is, in a way, wilful, but Apostasy is described as an extraordinary sin because of its seriousness — in that it is committed by a person who has been a member of a Christian church, not born again, but who knowingly and deliberately turns against the Lord. This is a real insult to Christ, who died a painful death for the salvation of a sinner. Unfortunately, for such a sinner, God has no other way of salvation. Rejection of the once-and-for-all sacrifice (Hebrews 10:26-29) leads to death because there will no other way of saving the sinner (Hebrews 6:4-6). Apostasy is not the same as backsliding. A backslider can be easily restored to Christ when he acknowledges Jesus Christ as Lord and Saviour.

When some believers today face really big challenges, they tend to think it's because they have drifted away from Christ and are now in apostasy. This is not true. This thinking is from the devil, and it is at times a misunderstanding of Hebrews 6:4-5. A person in apostasy does not have regret for drifting away from Christ.

When a person has not received the Grace of God, apostasy will be the result. Such a person hears the Gospel of Grace being preached, but, because of the sinful nature of the person's heart, the word cannot develop roots into the person's heart, like the seed on the rocky ground in Matthew 13:20-21.

With most young people, persecution and life challenges come as peer pressure and anti-Christ arguments from friends and adults they meet at colleges, universities, and workplaces. The result is that someone will willingly say goodbye to Christ the Saviour, like Judas Iscariot did.

There should be really no room for such a sin. New people who come to join a group of believers and are not yet saved need to be properly handled. They should be quickly taught how to walk in the truth of the Gospel. They need thorough, detailed, persistent teaching in the Gospel of Grace, the New Truth. A correct Christian foundation needs to be laid under the lives of these non-believers, who will have come to join believers. If this is not done, apostasy will be the result.

If you read through the book of Hebrews, you will see that this is a sin that really grieves. A number of times in this Book of the

Bible, the Hebrew people are strongly and repeatedly warned about the danger of falling into this sin (Hebrews 2:1-3; Hebrews 6:4-5; Hebrews 10:26-29).

In this same book, this sin is given various names and descriptions:

- Hebrews 2:1 — It is described as: drifting away
- Hebrews 3:12 — It is described as: turning away
- Hebrews 6:6 — It is described as: falling away
- Hebrews 10:25 — It is described as: forsaking the assembly
- Hebrews 10:26 — It is described as: deliberate sin
- Hebrews 12:16 — It is described as: selling one's inheritance
- Hebrews 12:25 — It is described as: refusing Him

The Apostle Paul knew very well about the problem of apostasy. How did he try to minimise it? Read Acts 14:21-28 and Acts 20:31. Paul spent a lot of time with people, helping to give them a good grounding in the Gospel of Grace. He was *feeding* them on Grace. If people are not being fed on Grace, they will feed themselves on rubbish, and they will become easy targets of the devil. The Bible says that apostasy will increase in the end times. See 1 Peter 4:1 and 2 Thessalonians 2:3.

This is a challenge to all believers today. What are we doing to minimise the sin of apostasy?

False Teachers

"I know that after I leave, savage wolves will come in among you and will not spare the flock. Even from your own number, men will rise and distort the truth in order to draw away disciples after them." (Acts 20:29-30).

False teachers, as the above passage says, are people who operate within the church, They appear like true ministers of the Gospel, but they mix truth and false information to lead people astray.

They will say some good and some true things about Jesus but deny that He is God. They will deny that He is the sole and sufficient Saviour of all people. They will deny that Jesus' death was a substitute for sinners. They will deny salvation by Grace through faith.

False teachers are not born-again people. They are just good public speakers, but, in truth, they will be saying nothing.

What false teachers say does not build up God's people. What they say destroys God's people. They lower Biblical moral standards and promote things of the flesh.

False teachers talk a lot about things related to sexual activities and show a great desire for money.

Darby J .N., in the book *The Collected Writings of John*, says, "The devil is never more satanic than when he carries a Bible". We see a similar picture in the Garden of Eden: The devil himself trying to talk theology — *"You will not surely die,"* said the devil to the woman (Genesis 3:4).

We see a complete distortion of God's word, and, unfortunately, those who embrace the distorted word of God will surely die.

Here is another really big challenge that faces the church of today:

Scoffers

These are people who do not fear God. They doubt and question most things said in the Bible. For example, they greatly doubt the Second Coming of our Lord Jesus Christ. *"Where is this coming he promised?"* (2 Peter 3:4), they ask.

Their argument is that, since the time of their forefathers, the Second Coming of Jesus has been talked about — so when is he coming? They encourage people to live as they please.

For believers to be able to withstand false teachers, scoffers and apostasy, they need to be continuously fed on the Gospel of Grace. This is the only thing that builds and empowers the believer.

CHAPTER 6

Empty Church Benches

Christian places of worship (church buildings) are easy to recognize from afar. They are normally large buildings with distinct external structural shapes and features. In most towns or cities, you will see a church building every few streets. Come Sunday morning, if you visit one of these places of worship, in most of these places, what you will see are several empty church benches (pews).

The few numbers of the congregation present will be the elderly pensioners and one or two grandchildren. The question to ask is, "So how do these small congregations, made up of mostly the elderly, manage to keep these massive church buildings open and functioning? How do these small congregations manage to sustain the other church activities, such as mission work? The truth is that most of these congregations are really struggling financially and from lack of manpower, especially in church activities that require higher skills, such as playing the piano.

What could be the solution? One would be to close the very small places of worship and make its members move on to join one of the other nearby places of worship. The other way around this problem might be to negotiate for a merger of two or three denominations to form one large denomination. These might appear like solutions, but the truth is that these are cosmetic changes — human effort dealing with a spiritual issue.

I am sure the solution could be found by looking at how the church started, how it was sustained then, and how is it being sustained today.

Origin and Nature of the Church

The Bible tells us that, up to Pentecost times, there were only two groups of people on earth, the Jews and the Gentiles. And then our Lord Jesus came onto this scene and established the third group of people, called the Church, the new creation, the new man, the Christian.

What is the church? When Christ dwells in a person, that person is the church. That is a very simple way of defining a church, but that definition has most of the features of what the Bible calls 'a church'. A more detailed definition, one that will help to explain the empty church benches is 'A church is an organism born of the Holy Spirit; it survives and thrives by the Holy Spirit only and not by human effort. The life and energy needed by the church to exist, to grow, and to function comes from the Holy Spirit. He and he alone gives life to the church, and, since Christ is the spirit, if you have no Christ, you have no life (1 John 5:12), and if there is no life, there is no church.

The church is not a building but a body or organism that came into being by the work of the indwelling Holy Spirit; it thrives on the Life, Energy/ Power, Guidance, and Cleansing of the Holy Spirit. If the Holy Spirit (Christ) is not present or is not allowed total control of the church, then that church will not grow, it will not have transforming power, and it will not have a real effect or a meaningful impact in this world. So it is not a luxury to have the Holy Spirit — it is a *must* for every believer. In the Bible, we read about Samson and Delilah (Judges 16:1-22). This story clearly shows that when the spirit of God is not at work in the life of a person, that person will be powerless and ineffective. When the spirit of God is not allowed total control of all activities of the church congregation, the church can preach, teach, help the poor, talk, plan, try this, and try that. But the truth is that such a church will slowly turn into a religious club and then die, as shown by many empty church benches we see when some congregations meet for Sunday service, Bible study, or other church functions.

Solution to the Empty Church Benches

The massive and numerous church buildings we see all over in some countries clearly show that, once upon a time, there were large denominations, with large congregations. So what has gone wrong?

Changes in the Pulpit

If any meaningful change is to take place in the Christian community, so as to radically improve on the very small congregations and bring life back into the once-dynamic congregations, then that change has to start in the pulpit — that is, with the preachers. What do they preach? How do they preach whenever they stand in front of the congregation? One major weakness in some pulpits is preaching that is done to please the congregation (see Galatians 1:10) or preaching that makes the message acceptable to the congregation and not preaching based on the message given by the Holy Spirit. This kind of preaching is the very opposite of the message of the Cross, and it tries to feed the sheep on something that has no spiritual value.

The common message you hear in a number of church services and in the Christian community in general is 'performance-based Christianity'. But the truth is, there is no such thing as performance-based Christianity. God's children gather every Sunday to be fed on the Gospel of Grace. They need to be constantly reminded that we are saved by Grace and sustained by Grace. The works we do don't bring us salvation. It is salvation that makes us do good works (Ephesians 2:8-10). This is what the Gospel of Grace teaches. Anything preached or taught to people that is the opposite of the Gospel of God's Grace has no power to transform people's lives, has no power to build up the people of God and has no power to enable them to live lives that give glory to Christ, as well as to live and walk in the truth of the Gospel (Galatians 2:14).

A congregation that is fed on the message opposite to the Gospel of Jesus will be a very spiritually weak congregation. It will have no power to attract new members, it will have no power to with stand against the devil, and, slowly, the devil will devour members of that congregation. The result will be that church congregations will become smaller and smaller. How are new members brought in into the church? It is by the work of the Holy Spirit and not by human effort. When we have anointed preachers in our pulpits, and when these anointed preachers preach the Gospel of Grace, watch what happens. Read Acts 2:41 and Acts 13:38-44. *3000* new believers were added by the Holy Spirit in Acts 2 and in Acts 13!

Paul preached the Gospel of Grace, and the whole town came to listen to him. When the Gospel of Grace is being preached, the spirit of God will move into people's hearts, convicting them of sin and leading them to repentance and accepting Jesus Christ as Lord and Saviour.

The Bible tells us the gift of prophecy is a gift that preachers must desire, but they are not to receive any new revelations from God, because God has completed all there is for us to know in the Bible. But preachers are prophets in the sense that these are men and women who preach the Gospel of Jesus Christ with boldness, with authority, like Apostle Paul in chains in front of King Agrippa (Acts 26:1-32). At one point, they had to stop him, saying, *"Your great learning is driving you insane"* (also see Matthew 7:29). Such preaching results in edification, which is the building up of God's people (the church). *"But he who prophesies edifies the church"* (1 Corinthians 14:3-5). If preaching fails to edify the church, then preachers have failed. Is this not what has happened in churches that we see closing because the membership has shrunk so drastically? The gift of prophecy has a key role in leading non-believers to Christ and in building up believers so that they can live lives that glorify Christ.

Through the Holy Spirit, preachers receive what they have to take to the people. Thus, preachers must learn to receive from God. Otherwise they will have nothing to give to the congregation. What the preacher receives from God to take to the congregation is not just words; it is words packed with the power of God. Look at Jonah, the man we read about in the Bible. He did not want to go to Nineveh, but when he finally agreed, all he did when he got to Nineveh was to speak very few words, a very short sermon. *"Forty more days and Nineveh will be overturned"* (Jonah 3:4).

But because it was a message that carried with it the convicting power of God's Holy Spirit, what was the result? Jonah 3:5 tells us, *"The Ninevites believed God."* Salvation came to Nineveh. All that Jonah was required to do was to speak the words of God specifically for Nineveh, much in the same manner as there were specific messages for the seven churches in Revelation 2 and 3, and in 1 Peter 4:11. Jonah did not speak words that were meant to gain him favour from the people of Nineveh. He just proclaimed the words of God, and the spirit of God took over, applied the message to the hearts of the people, and they repented. Does this not shed some light on how God's revival starts? Revival is the work of God, and the finished work of Christ at Calvary has made available to us all that is required for the revival of the whole world.

The spirit of God is ready to move in a large scale upon people. What is needed is men and women who say 'Yes' to God, who say goodbye to everything like the Apostle Paul (Philippians 3:7-11), to be filled with the grace and spirit of God, pray without ceasing, and preach the Gospel of Grace boldly. There will be mass movement of the spirit of God, just as we saw in the Welsh revival of 1904-1905. Conversion to Christianity is just the beginning of the Christian journey. The new believers need a lot of support and encouragement. In the Bible, in the book of Acts, we read about the Apostle Paul visiting and revisiting believers in various places and sometimes staying with them for a very long time, teaching them the Gospel of Jesus Christ.

This greatly helped to strengthen and encourage old and new believers (Acts 14:22). After Pentecost and after the Welsh revival, we still saw people lapsing spiritually as time went by. To control this, more teachers and teaching resources to take people into deeper understanding of God are needed. Do we see anything like this today? What arrangements are in place in churches to promote real, meaningful spiritual growth? A one-hour Sunday service cannot cover much ground.

Note: Spiritual lapse comes about because people have a great desire for independence. The Holy Spirit will not be allowed full control of such people.

Church membership is also greatly affected by church policies. Some churches have greatly conformed blithely to the patterns of the world — especially on what constitutes sin. There are some denominations in which some types of sin are classified as human rights. Yet this is why Jesus died (1 Peter 3:18). Is this not an insult to Christ? The Bible has clearly stated what sin is (Romans 1:18-32; 2 Timothy 3:1-17). The question is: Why would the Holy Spirit add new members to denominations in which Christians are fed on human rights instead of on the Gospel of Grace? The spirit of God will add new members only where people are being pointed to Christ and are being built up to be people who live lives that glorify Christ. Where Christ is glorified, growth takes place.

Judaising the Church

Chapters 3 and 7 of this book speak at length about the move from Judaism to Christianity and the formation of the church. In this book, the church has been described as a new organism that never existed before, with nothing in it of Judaism and nothing in it from the Gentile life. But, sadly, some church congregations have adopted many features/aspects of Judaism. This has robbed the church of its power, and, thus, there has been no growth. Dr. C. I. Schofield, in the book *Rightly Dividing the Word of Truth*, says 'It may be safely said that the Judaising of the church has done more to hinder her progress, pervert her mission, and destroy her spiritually than all other causes combined. Instead of pursuing her appointed path of separation from the world and following the Lord in her heavenly calling, she has used Jewish scriptures to justify herself in lowering her purpose to the civilization of the world, the acquisition of wealth, the use of an imposing ritual, the erection of magnificent churches… and the division of equal brotherhood into 'clergy and 'laity'.

CHAPTER 7

The Major Biblical Covenants

"This is the covenant I will make with the house of Israel after that time, declares the lord. I will put my laws in their minds and write them on their hearts. I will be their God, and they will be my people. No longer will a man teach his neighbour or a man his brother, saying, "Know the lord" because they will all know me, from the least to the greatest. For I will forgive their wickedness and remember their sins no more" (Hebrews 8:10-12).

The Bible passage quoted above is what is called the New Covenant or the Covenant of Grace or simply, 'Grace'.

This is one of the major covenants we find in the Bible. Covenants form key the components of god's dispensation. A dispensation is God's way of administrating his affairs with people at a particular time.

What is a covenant? And how was it arrived at? In the Bible, a covenant is a permanent agreement between God and his people. In Biblical times, when you 'covenant' with someone, you bring an animal — a ram or a goat — and kill it by cutting it in two. The two pieces of the animal would be placed a few feet or centimetres apart. Then the two people entering into the covenant would face each other, walk towards each other between the two cut pieces of the animal, and continue past each other in opposite directions.

This bound both parties to protect and provide for each other. In the covenant between God and man, God has everything, and man has nothing, so the one that benefits is the poorer party. Our God is able to keep up with the requirements on the covenant, but man cannot. So, to make sure the covenant does not fail, Jesus represented us in the cutting of the New Covenant. God the Father and God the Son cut the New Covenant at Calvary. The same thing happened in the covenant between God and Abraham (Genesis 15:8-21). Jesus appeared as the pillar of fire and cut the covenant with God the Father, who appeared as the pillar of cloud. Jesus represented Abraham.

Biblical Covenants

1. Noahic Covenant

This is a covenant made between God and Noah. God promises never again to destroy all life on Earth (Genesis 9:8-17). This was after the flood that killed all life on Earth in the time of Noah.

2. Abrahamic Covenant

The Abrahamic covenant is found in the book of Genesis, Chapters 12-17. There are three covenants God made with Abraham. In Genesis 12:1-3, God promises to make Abraham a great nation and make his name great. In Genesis 15:8-21, God promises Abraham's descendants land from the river of Egypt to the Great river of Euphrates. In Genesis 17:2-9, God promises to make Abraham the father of many nations and of many descendants; circumcision is the permanent sign of this everlasting covenant with Abraham and his descendants.

3. Mosaic Covenant

This was a covenant between God and the Children of Israel. It was given by God through angels to Moses to pass on to the Children of Israel (Hebrews 2:2). This covenant is found in the following books of the Bible: Exodus, Leviticus, Numbers, and Deuteronomy.

In this covenant, God promises to make Israel His earthly chosen people (Exodus 19:5) and a kingdom of priests and a holy nation (Exodus 19:6). This was on the condition that the Children of Israel obeyed God's commandments.

4. Priestly Covenant

This was a covenant that God made with Aaron and his descendants. It was the covenant that created the Aaronic priesthood (Exodus 28).

5. Davidic Covenant

This was a covenant that established David and his descendants as the kings of the nation of the whole of Israel, (2 Samuel 7).

6. The New Covenant

Derived from Jeremiah 31:31-34 and Hebrews 8:10-12, it is a covenant that talks about the Messianic age (Jesus Christ); God promises to forgive people's sins, to put His laws into people's hearts, and to be

God to His people. It is all about God's Grace.

The Two Major Covenants

The two major covenants are the Old Covenant (The Law) and the New Covenant (Grace).

In this book, we will talk about the Old Covenant and the New Covenant, or The Law and Grace.

Many people know the Ten Commandments (the Old Covenant) fairly well. Some people go on to say that they have a right standing before God because they know the Ten Commandments. I have also seen some wall plaques of the Ten Commandments hanging in some people's houses and in some school buildings. I always wonder if the people in these places know why the Law was given in the first place and what the Law can and cannot do in a person's life.

People often use the phrase 'New Covenant,' but if you ask them what the New Covenant is all about, many Christians will struggle to give you a straightforward answer. Yet they are talking about the New Covenant every time they talk about Jesus and His finished work.

The Old Covenant/The Law

The Children of Israel, on their way from Egypt to the Promised Land, clearly show that, although they were out of Egypt, their hearts must have still been full of Egyptian ways of life. This is shown by the fact that, every time they faced a challenge on their way to the Promised Land, their cry was not to be taken quickly to the Promised

Land of Milk and Honey. Their cry was to be taken back to Egypt (Numbers 14:4; Exodus 16:3). It is clear that the Children of Israel did not have a revelation that Canaan and all the good in it should be their destination. All they had in their hearts was Egypt — despite its hardships.

At Mount Sinai (Exodus 19:1-8), God begins to introduce Himself and reveal His nature more clearly to His earthly chosen people (the Jews). It looks like God's intention was to bring his people into His presence so that He could reveal Himself to them and impart Himself as a loving, holy God into them through his speaking to them. The way God chose to do this was to speak through Moses. In Exodus 34:28-29, Moses was with God for 40 days and 40 nights. During that lengthy time, God must have been speaking to Moses, and Moses must have been thoroughly infused with God and saturated with Him. This could explain why Moses face shone (Exodus 34:35).

Before God gave the Law to Moses, God must have intended to give Himself to him, and I am sure this is what God was trying to do with the Children of Israel. Unfortunately, the Children of God did not know God, and they also did not know themselves.

They must have thought God wanted them to do certain things for Him. Sadly, they thought that, whatever God wanted them to do, they could easily do it, using their human effort. Exodus 19:8 clearly shows their thinking: *"We will do everything the Lord has said."*

They did not know what or were not aware of the details of what God was going to do or say, but, already, they were quick to say that they could do whatever God wanted them to do.

God then gave them the Ten Commandments/The Law. What

was the result? Exodus Chapter 32 relates the incident involving the golden calf. The Children of Israel broke the very first Commandment — despite having promised God that they would do whatever He wanted them to do. The sad part of the Law is that, by breaking one aspect of the Law, you become guilty of breaking all of the Law (James 2:10). The penalty for breaking just one aspect of the Law was death (Galatians 3:10 and Numbers 15:32-36).

The Old Covenant was an administrative system given to the Children of Israel. It was based on conditional promises: A person was blessed for obeying the Law but also punished for breaking the Law (Hebrews 2:2). The main emphasis in the Law was on what men were to do. It was all about people doing something, and yet these people were not empowered to do what the Law demanded. This made it an inferior covenant. It was also inferior in two other ways: 1) It failed to remove sin — it only covered sin for a limited period (Hebrews 10:1-4); and 2) It was given through a servant of God (Moses) and not the Son of God (Jesus).

The Old Covenant itself is good, but people failed to do what they had promised (Exodus 19:8; Exodus 24:4).

The Old Covenant was made up of the Moral Law and the Ceremonial Law.

The Major Aspects of the Law

The Ten Commandments were written on stone tablets (Exodus 20:1-20)

1) Miscellaneous law (Exodus Chapters 21-24)

2) Animal and grain offering (Leviticus Chapters 1-7)

3) Feasts and festivals (Exodus 23:14-19; Leviticus 23:1-44)

4) The priests and their garments (Exodus Chapters 28-29)

5) Circumcision (Genesis 17:11)

6) Keeping the Sabbath (Exodus 31:12-18)

7) Clean foods and unclean foods (Leviticus Chapter 11)

8) The Tabernacle and all the furniture in it (Exodus Chapters 26 and 36-38

Note: The Old Covenant is what is referred to as the 'Old Truth' in this book. It was the truth before our Lord Jesus Christ came. Now that He has come, it is no longer the truth. This 'Old Truth' is referred to in the Bible as "*obsolete*" (Hebrews 8:13).

What God Never Meant the Purpose of the Law to Be

1) The Law was never meant to be the way of salvation (Romans 3:21-22).

2) The Law was never meant to be a way of obtaining God's righteousness (Romans 3:20).

3) The Law was never meant to be a way of worship or a rule of life once Grace had come or once a person had accepted Jesus Christ as Lord and Saviour (Romans 6: 14). The Law today remains a rule of worship or a rule of life for the Jews, who have not accepted Jesus Christ.

4) The Law was never meant to completely remove a person's sins but just to cover sin for a limited period (Hebrews 10:1-4).

5) The Law was never meant to empower a person or to enable a person to observe the Law (Romans 3:20).

6) The Law was never meant for Gentiles (Exodus 19:1-6; Exodus 31:12-13

What Was the Purpose of the Law?

1) The Law was given to keep, guard, and teach the Israelites on things acceptable to God until the coming of Christ (Galatians 3:24).

2) The Law was given to point people to Christ (Galatians 3:24).

3) The Law was given to reveal the sinful nature of people and to demonstrate that people were sinners, with external and internal sin (Romans 3:20).

4) The Law given was to show that sin is a transgression — a violation of a known regulation (Romans 7:7).

5) The Law was put in place to show that all people need a Saviour (Galatians 3:24).

6) The Law was given to be a shadow or picture, a 'type' ('typology') of Christ; the Law was given to represent Christ (Hebrews 10:1).

The above shows us that the Law is only a shadow of Christ. It has no power to regenerate a person, it has no power to transform a person into a new creation, and it is not able to break the power of sin. This makes it an inferior covenant. Is it not sad to see that today some people are abandoning Christ, the only reality, and going back to the Law, the shadow, which has no power to transform a person's life? Is this not an insult to Christ, who went through that very painful death on the Cross to bring us salvation? It is necessary to take seriously the warning given in Hebrews 10:29, which says *"How much more severely do you think a man deserves to be punished who trampled the Son of God under foot, who treated as an unholy thing the blood of the covenant that sanctified him, and who has insulted the Spirit of grace?"*

There are people today who believe they get a right standing before God by keeping the Sabbath, by observing certain feasts and festivals, by observing holy places, by using holy water, by putting on a church uniform, or by using priestly garments, with all their decorations.

All these things have been brought into Christianity from Judaism.

They just dilute Christianity. They rob the Cross of its power (1 Corinthians 1:17). It is like putting new wine into old skins. The things that have been brought into Christianity from Judaism were just shadows of Christ. Today, Christ has come, and He is the fulfilment of the whole Law, and His finished work on the Cross has satisfied all the requirements of God for a believer to have a right standing before God. So all these things mentioned above have no value in Christianity. They are part of the 'Old truth'. They are obsolete.

The Bible calls the Law 'a shadow' (Hebrews 10:1), 'weak and useless' (Hebrews 7:18-19, and 'the ministry of death' (2 Corinthians 3:7).

The question is: Why depend on that which is called the 'ministry of death' by the Bible? Why depend on 'a shadow' when the reality is there for the living? It is like a man who spends most of his time admiring and talking to his wife's photograph when the wife, the real person, is right next to him — and he's not talking to her.

In view of this, should we preach/teach the Law? The answer is 'Yes, we must preach/teach the Law. It is a part of the Bible that shows one of the major dispensations of God. We must preach/teach the Law as one of the major things that point to the coming of Christ. So, the Law must be preached on, but only with the aim of using it as a pointer to Christ.

A few more 'shadows' of Christ that we see in the Bible are:

• Animal and grain offerings were used for atonement of sin. These were repeated, year in, year out. They were a picture of Christ's once-and-for- all sacrifice for sin.

- Another 'shadow' of Christ in the Tabernacle is the top cover of the Ark of the Covenant. It was called the 'mercy seat'. It was an atonement cover, covering over the sins of the people through the yearly atonement sacrifice performed by the high priest in the Holy of Holies. The mercy seat was a picture of Christ who was coming to cover and take away people's sins.

- The table of showbread was a picture Christ, the Bread of Life.

- The golden lamp stand was a picture of Christ as the light of the world.

- The Ark of the Covenant itself was a 'shadow'. The gold on it symbolised Christ's deity, and the wood on it symbolised Christ's humanity.

The New Covenant

The New Covenant/Grace is the 'New Truth', and this is what all believers should be in step with.

The New Covenant came directly from our Lord Jesus. It is a covenant based on God's grace, with unconditional promises.

According to the New Covenant, when a person believes in Jesus, he/she is forgiven of all sins, past, present, and future, and, at the same time, the believer is covered with God's righteousness. Grace teaches a believer how to live a Godly life (Titus 2:11-12). Grace breaks the power in and over the believer's life, Grace empowers a believer to live a Godly life, and Grace rewards believers for the good they do.

What Are the Good Unconditional Promises of the New Covenant?

It is a covenant based on what God will do and not on what a person must do (Hebrews 8:10).

God will impart His life into a person's heart. This gives the believer the nature of God and the ability to know and love God (Hebrews 8:10-11).

It promises a reconciliation of man to God and the formation of a close, unending relationship between God and man (Hebrews 8:10). Because of this reconciliation, all believers will free to approach God at any time (Hebrews 4:16).

At the Second Coming of Jesus, the New Covenant will be universal in nature, and everyone will have an inward knowledge of God (Hebrews 8:11).

It promises forgiveness of sins and God not remembering them anymore Hebrews 8:12.

The New Covenant is an unconditional agreement of Grace between God and His earthly chosen people, the Jews, which is to be fully implemented at the Second Coming of our Lord Jesus, when He sets up His kingdom on earth. During that time, the nation of Israel will be fully restored and redeemed.

In the meantime (today), believers — Gentiles and Jews — enjoy some of the benefits of this covenant, for example, a free supply of forgiveness of sins, having a relationship with God (*reconciled to God*), a free supply of Grace.

Comparisons Between the New and Old Covenants

New Covenant	Old Covenant
It is spiritual, based on what God has, is, and will do	It is carnal, based on what man must do
Makes a believer know about salvation	Makes a person know about sin
Given by the Son of God (Jesus) directly to the people (Hebrews 2:3)	Given through a servant of God (Moses) (Hebrews 2:2)
Unconditional promises, blessings freely given to a believer	Conditional promises, blessings only to those who obey the law
Grace imparts righteousness onto a believer (Hebrews 8:6)	Law demands righteousness from a person
Grace teaches and empowers a believer to live a Godly life (Titus 2:11-12)	Law demands that a person lives a Godly life, but it does not empower a person to live such a life
Grace rewards those who live a Godly life	Law punishes those who fail to obey
Sins removed and forgiven (Hebrews 8:12)	Sins just covered for a limited period
It is there forever	It is temporary
Worldwide in application	Local application for Jews only

Covenants and Priesthood

A covenant and priesthood go hand in hand. The Aaronic priesthood and all the priestly garments were part of the old covenant.

The priesthood of Jesus is part of the New Covenant.

Comparisons Between the Priesthood of Jesus and the Aaronic Priesthood

Priesthood of Jesus	Aaronic Priesthood
Priest in the order of Melchizedek (Hebrews 7:17)	Priest in the order of Aaron (Hebrews 7:11)
Superior, perfect priesthood (Hebrews 7:11)	Imperfect, weak priesthood (Hebrews 7:28)
Priest with an oath, so guarantee of a better covenant (Hebrews 7:21-22)	Priest with no oath. The law made nothing perfect (Hebrews 7:19-20)
Priest on the basis of divine life (Hebrews 7:16)	Priest on the basis of ancestry regulation (Hebrews 7:16)
Priest perfect, blameless, holy (Hebrews 7:26)	Weak priest, with sin (Hebrews 7:26-27)
Priest forever (Hebrews 7:17)	Temporary priest; death prevented priests from remaining in office forever (Hebrews 7:23)

Our Lord Jesus came to transfer people from the Old Covenant to the New Covenant. Living under the New Covenant is being in step with God. Living under a mixture of Law and Grace is not being in step with God and is not walking in the truth of the Gospel. So, what is walking in the Truth of the Gospel? Living under Grace and Grace alone is living in the Truth of the Gospel.

CHAPTER 8

Christ in Me

"I am again in pain...until Christ is formed in you" (Galatians 4:19). The first time we meet the Apostle Paul in the Bible, he was called 'Saul', and he showed a high level of physical aggression towards the church. He worked hard to destroy the church, but in the Bible passage quoted above, we see the same person — still full of zeal and determination — but this time, it is directed towards building up the church, not using physical force but under the power of the Holy Spirit. In the passage above, Paul uses the words *"pain"* and *"until Christ is formed in you"*. This shows how the mighty power of God had greatly transformed Paul into a man full of deep, divine love that pushed him to the extent of being in *"pain"* for wanting to see other believers transformed like him, to be Christ-like. The Apostle Paul was not satisfied with people remaining as baby Christians.

He desired to see them transformed into mature Christians. This Bible passage also shows that Christ, the living person, is the main focus of Paul's gospel and for this wonderful Christ to be in the believer.

This also explains why Paul remained at one place with believers, strengthening them, encouraging them, teaching and preaching to them about the mystery of Christ or the Gospel of God's Grace. This, I am sure, greatly helped believers to get a clear picture of Christ and his finished work. The result of this was spiritual growth, and the believer would begin to show Christ-like characteristics. When this happened, Paul would say that Christ was being formed in the believer.

Such a believer does not show a compartmentalised life. What type of life is 'compartmentalised'? They are believers who show a form of Christian life which is in clear-cut segments: Time for worship is Sunday 10:00 am to 11:00 am — and that's it. The next time they come near a Bible is the following Sunday. In between, they live a life completely independent of God. They do not involve God in their family life — well, maybe once or twice during infant baptism and burial of a cousin. They work for their families independent of God, they entertain the family, and they generally live their lives not in the truth of the gospel. The diagram below shows a picture of a believer who lives a compartmentalised life.

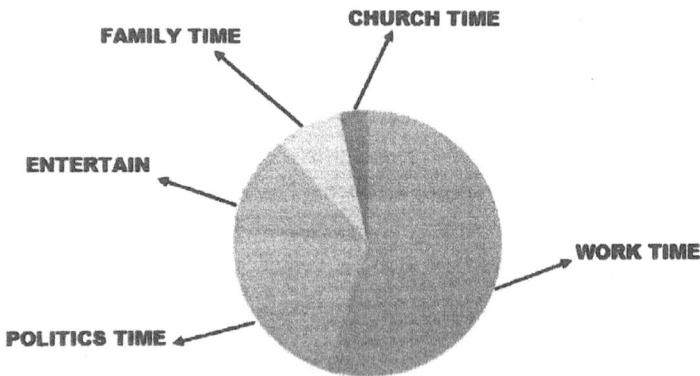

BUT WE NEED TO REMEMBER THAT CHRIST'S DESIRES IS TO BE ALL, AND IN ALL.

When Christ is formed in the believer, the divine life now in the believer is supposed to transform the compartmentalised human life into one unit with Christ, making Christ the centre of every aspect of a believer's life. By so doing, Christ will express Himself in and through every aspect of the believer's life. At work, it will be Christ working through the believer. At home, with the family, Christ will be the centre of all that takes place in the family. Praying, praising God, thanking God, Bible study, and fellowshipping with other believers all become a daily and normal way of living. Does the world see Christ at work in every aspect of our daily lives? If our Christ-likeness is seen on Sunday only, then we are not living according to the truth of the Gospel.

God's desire for all believers is that Christ will be born in the believer, that Christ will be allowed to live in a believer, and that Christ will be allowed to fill the heart and soul of the believer as divine life, so that the believer does exhibit the nature of Christ. Today, Christ desires to live in the heart of every believer — Jew and Gentile alike. In Biblical times, people thought that Christ could enter the heart of a Jew, but no one ever thought that could happen with a Gentile. But today, this is happening. This is what Paul calls the *mystery of Christ*.

In Ephesians 3:6, the Bible says, *"this mystery is that, through the Gospel, the Gentiles are heirs together with Israel, members together of one body, and sharers together in the promise in Christ Jesus"*. From this, we see that Paul came not to announce doctrines but to announce the riches of Christ. What are the 'riches of Christ'? The riches of Christ are all that He is to us: Christ is our life, righteousness, holiness, redemption, and much more. The riches of Christ are what *He* has for us, and what He accomplished, attained, and obtained for us.

This Christ, with all His riches, now dwells in the spirit of a believer — as life and as a person. To the Gentile, this is really a mystery, but, above all, He is the hope of glory, that is, an assurance of going to heaven, for believers. Before Jesus Christ came into this world, there were two classes of people — Jews and Gentiles — and there was hostility between these two classes of people. Our Lord Jesus came and introduced another class of people — the church, the new man. What does this mean? It means that both Jews and Gentiles are reconciled to God and to one another, eliminating, removing, and abolishing the hostility between them (Ephesians 2:13-22). It also shows that the church was a completely new organism formed by the work of the Holy Spirit at Pentecost. The church, being a new organism that had never existed before, meant that the church was and is to have nothing of Judaism in it and nothing of the Gentile way of life in it.

The church is supposed to be all about Christ, and Christ alone. This is the way believers are reconciled to God and to one another, because God, who is love and has enabling power, will now be living in a believer. This enables Jewish believers to love Gentile believers. Tolerating people who are very different from themselves enables Christians to forgive and love those who hate them, doing away with things like racism, tribalism, and anti-Semitism.

When He is allowed to take over the whole life of a believer, Christ, because of His glorious riches, produces a real new man, able to love and forgive the most difficult people. Because of Christ, all believers — Jews *and* Gentiles alike — become part of the body of Christ. With Christ Himself as the head of the body of all believers — Jews and Gentiles — become equal in the eyes of God. This must be God's greatest desire.

Christ, and Christ alone, in us is more than sufficient for a person to be recognized, to be seen, to be known, or to function very effectively as a Christian. But some Christians view church uniforms, priestly garments, church attendance, church positions, church duties, and giving to the poor as ways of becoming a good or a better Christian. They view these things as a way of getting a right standing before God. This is an insult to Christ and His finished work.

NOTE: The Bible says that our own righteousness (not our sin) is like filthy rags in the eyes of God (Isaiah 64:6).

The danger of some of these things is they compete with Christ in affection and loyalty in the believer's heart. Anything that competes with Christ is the work of the devil. After accepting Jesus as Lord, as the almighty, in ones life, if a believer then goes on to consider human effort as necessary to improve on the finished work of Christ, then there is a problem. For such believers, the Bible has a strong warning, in Hebrews 10:29. Such a person is guilty of three things:

- *"Trampling the Son of God underfoot,*
- *counting the blood of covenant by which one is sanctified as a   common thing, and*
- *insulting the spirit of grace."*

The sufficiency of Christ over the entire life of a believer reminds me of the time I caught malaria fever. When the parasite that causes malaria fever was in me, there was nothing I could do to show the signs and symptoms of malaria fever. The parasite in me was the one that caused my body to show signs and symptoms of malaria fever. The same applies to Christianity. Christ in a believer is the sole and sufficient requirement for Christ-like characteristics to be shown through a believer and not human effort.

Christ's sufficiency is enough for a believer to be a Christ-like husband, wife, parent, pastor, politician, etc. Christ's sufficiency in every aspect of a believer's life must be taken seriously and greatly honoured.

In 2 Timothy 3:10-12, the Apostle Paul shows the sufficiency of Christ is more than enough for a believer to live a true Christian life. Paul arrived at this level of Christianity by abandoning all that he grew up putting a lot of value in — things like Judaism and self-right-eousness. He did this to gain Christ, to have Christ living in him, and to have Christ formed in him.

His Christian life shows that Christ was indeed formed in him. He travelled widely, preaching and teaching the Gospel of Grace. His travels are clearly shown in the book of Acts as 'The journeys of Paul'. He faced a lot of persecution. To those who persecuted him, he showed love and preached the Gospel of Jesus to them whenever they gave him a chance. In spite of the many challenges, he still managed to write thirteen books of the New Testament — and some of these, he wrote while in prison. The work done by Paul clearly shows what happens when Christ lives in a person.

Let us listen to what Paul said about his life: "I consider my life worth nothing more to me, if only I may finish the race and complete the task the Lord Jesus has given me, the task of testifying to the gospel of God's grace" (Acts 20:24). It can only be Christ who was in Paul who was making him do and say all that.

Reading through Hebrews Chapter 11, we see that people who lived under the law achieved quite a lot. They are listed in the Bible as great people of faith. Should this not be a challenge to the Christian of today? The Christian of today has Christ in him/her — Christ with all His glorious riches and Christ with all His superior qualities (Hebrews Chapters 1-9). Christ is the embodiment of the fullness of the Godhead (Colossians 2:9). Christ the reality of all shadows (the Law) we read about in the Old Testament (Hebrews 10:1 and Colossians 2:16-17).

So, believers having Christ in them are expected to do much more and make a far-greater impact on the world than the people who lived under the Law.

Living with the King of Kings

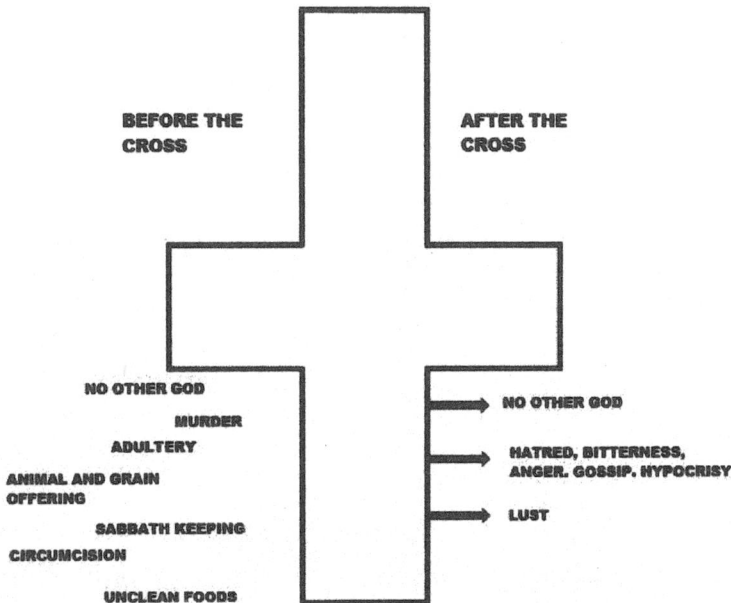

BEFORE THE CROSS

AFTER THE CROSS

NO OTHER GOD

MURDER

ADULTERY

ANIMAL AND GRAIN OFFERING

SABBATH KEEPING

CIRCUMCISION

UNCLEAN FOODS

NO OTHER GOD

HATRED, BITTERNESS, ANGER, GOSSIP, HYPOCRISY

LUST

The above diagram shows what happens to the Law when a person accepts Jesus Christ, the King of Kings, as Lord and Saviour.

It is not good enough to say, 'I do not commit murder' and yet harbour in one's heart hatred, bitterness, anger, and gossip. In the eyes of God, murder is sin (external sin), and hatred, bitterness, anger, gossip, and unforgiveness also sin (internal sin). It is not good enough in the eyes of God to say, 'I do not commit adultery' and yet lust. Lust is internal sin. External sin and internal sin are all sin in the eyes of God, and a Saviour is needed for all forms of sin. When Christ came, he amplified the Law. See diagram below.

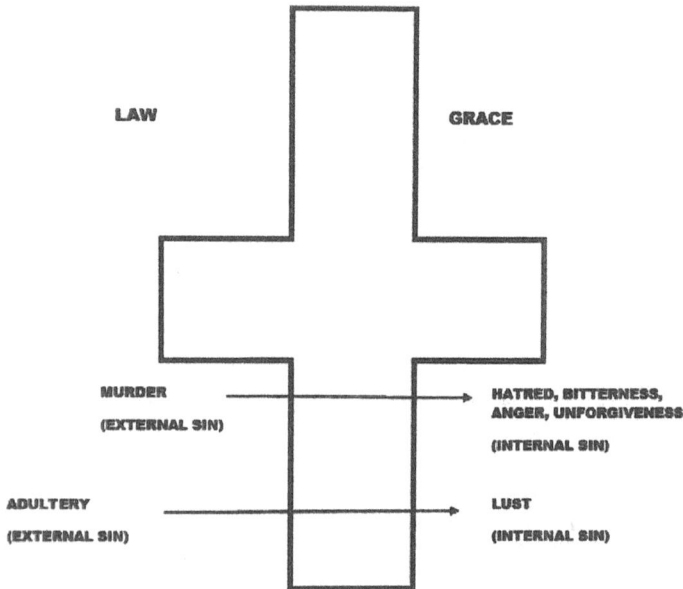

By amplifying the Law, Christ was clearly showing people that they are sinners. For example, one might say, 'I do not commit murder, so I am not a sinner'. But Christ is saying that, even though one might not commit murder, any bitterness in the heart of that person makes him/her a sinner. The above diagram also shows that it is not possible to live under the Law without breaking it. Human effort does not give the power required to observe the Law. The same is true with the

Christian life: One cannot use human effort to live a Christian life. One will totally fail to live a Christian life using human effort. Only God's power can enable a person to do what the Law demands, and only the Holy Spirit, Christ/God's Grace, will enable a person to live a Christian life. Today, the Holy Spirit comes only into a person who has accepted Jesus Christ as Lord and Saviour. So, again, we see that, when Christ, the King, comes to live in a person, only then can a person be a Christian and be victorious over sin.

Living with the King

A very good example of living with the King is found in 1 Samuel 22:1-2. We see David (the anointed king) running away from Saul. David ended up in the cave of Adullam; his relatives followed him and lived with him in the cave. The people who followed David were said to be in distress or in debt or discontented. These people, with all their problems, spent most of the time in the cave with the king (David) just worshipping and praising God. David wrote Psalm 34 during the time he was in the cave with his discontented men. The result of continuous worshipping and praising god was complete transformation of the sinful men who came to be with David into David's mighty men (2 Samuel 23).

The same will happen to any person who spends time with the King of Kings (Jesus). One's life will be greatly transformed and greatly blessed, and this is what the King of Kings (Jesus) came to do in this world. He will transform all who come to Him today from being religious people into Christians.

Let me end this book by quoting William Booth (10 April 1829-20 August 1912), Founder of the Salvation Army. This is how he responded to a question about modern-day dangers for the Christian church: "The chief danger that confronts the coming century will be religion without the Holy Spirit, Christianity without Christ, forgiveness without repentance, salvation without regeneration, politics without God, and heaven without hell."

CHRIST   IN   ME   CHURCH

2014

WALK IN THE TRUTH OF THE GOSPEL

www.ingramcontent.com/pod-product-compliance
Lightning Source LLC
Chambersburg PA
CBHW071617040426
42452CB00009B/1370